GOD
DID THAT

GOD DID THAT

Living the Grace Life

Rob Griffin

TATE PUBLISHING
AND ENTERPRISES, LLC

TABLE OF CONTENTS

THE JOURNEY BEGINS

What does it mean to live the Grace Life? This may be one of the most important questions we will ever ask. It is the type of question that sets your mind on a journey toward the destination of truth. But this is not just any journey. This is a journey into Kingdom Advance! While you read this text, I want to share with you some things that I have learned about grace and its powerful affect. My discovery, while attempting to answer the initial question, is that living the Grace Life means living your life in such a way that you set yourself in motion to be part of God's advancing Kingdom in this world.

In order to accomplish this we find that the Grace Life is living under the influence of God with his agenda in mind. This produces action in your life that has Kingdom ramifications. Living the Grace Life changes everything! At least it did for me.

I have not always known about the Grace Life— even though I was raised in a devoted Christian home. To start with, my dad did not attend church very often, but he loved the Lord and wanted his kids to be "in church." On the other hand, my mom was deeply devoted to church life. We went to church every time the doors were opened. Looking back, I remember experiencing a whole lot of church, but this was not just any church experience.

My mom was raised going to church in a holiness Pentecostal denomination and so were we—myself and my four siblings. It was full of emotional church services, demonstrative worship, and the expression of the Holy Spirit baptism and his gifts. I learned many good things in this environment including having a hunger for the supernatural and an expression of faith for the miraculous. It was there that I was taught to pray and to have a desire to serve the Lord with all of my heart. I also learned how to be sensitive to the voice of God and the gifts of the Spirit.

At the risk of offense, I must be honest about the other side of this experience. What follows is conveyed as a reflection from the confines of my own memory and personal perspective of the events that took place. I am no different than others in that I view the past through a personal paradigm. I am reflecting on how I saw it, how I felt at the time, and how I feel about it now. To be sure, I certainly don't want to offend in the opening remarks of this book so please bear with me as I touch the surface of a difficult reality from my past.

I have pondered often on my past experience. I have thought that it could be that I missed the teaching and emphasis on grace within the denomination and from the ministers that I was exposed to. In deeper retrospect, I have thought that maybe it was there under the surface but I didn't hear it. At the same time, I have also thought that maybe a clear directive concerning grace was not there at all. I have come to a point in my life where I believe that the most reasonable explanation for my lack of catching it is the result of there being such an emphasis on works that there was very little room left to focus on anything else!

The result for me was less grace and more self-works. Whatever may or may not have been taught, I remember rules. I remember being fearful that I wasn't doing enough. I remember constantly trying to do right and live a life of obedience that was tied to certain lifestyle rules that were imposed by the pulpit. Because of this, I felt like the favor of God was associated with my personal commitment to do certain things that were taught in the denomination. I also remember feeling unworthy. I could never do enough to please the preachers or to please God. It was as though I was doomed because I was too human.

I don't remember the Grace Life being taught with any emphasis at all. Matter of fact, I really don't remember much grace to speak of on any level. I realize now that I lived for God by works and I was trying to "feel" worthy of his love and salvation through them. I fell into a state of mind where everything about God's love and favor was contingent on what I did under my own ability and not on what Christ did for me.

This became even more evident when I realized that many of these "works" were done as a result of a cultural environment in the church that dictated them to me. I was taught this way of living from childhood and was told that I should accept it as God's bidding. There was no leading of the Holy Spirit. There doesn't seem to have been much of a chance for that.

I thought he was leading me, but in reality most of these things were done as a part of the church culture that was engrained in me as a child and as a standard of living practiced religiously among us. It was simply our lifestyle and a huge part of our identity as a sect of Christianity. We were very legalistic in this self-proclaimed "Apostolic Identity" which consisted of exclusive doctrines and holiness lifestyle codes. I found myself carrying this legalistic Christian ideology into the ministry and into my thirties!

Grace in those days was almost an "unheard of." Living for God had more to do with obeying the lifestyle regulations of the denomination (and how the pastors taught them) than it did about the grace of God working through me for Kingdom purpose. This may come across harsh which is not my intention, but you really don't need grace when you have preachers telling you exactly what to do, what to wear, how to act, and where to go at all times.

When lifestyle rules are clearly articulated in manuals and sermons that tell you how to dress and how to live in intricate detail, a Spirit led life is by and large unnecessary. I not only grew up in this way of thinking, I operated from this paradigm for the first sixteen years of personal ministry.

Allow me for a moment to give a brief snapshot of our ministerial history for the sake of timeline clarity in the subsequent chapters of this book—although I will visit some of this with more detail in later chapters. I began in ministry in 1986 at the age of nineteen in the great state of Texas. Beginning in 1987, I traveled full time in an evangelistic ministry as an itinerate preacher. In 1995, as my wife, Raylene, was expecting our first child, my father-in-law asked if we would come pastor with him in the South Tulsa area of Oklahoma at the church that Raylene had been raised in. We accepted that assignment and assisted him for almost three years.

In April of 1998, Raylene and I accepted a pastorate in Oklahoma City, Oklahoma. On a side note, this was a real stretch for this Texan seeing that we now pastored in Oklahoma City, in Oklahoma County, in the State of Oklahoma! It would appear that I had really crossed north over the Red River! At this point, all I needed was to find a house on Oklahoma Street, and I am sure that my Texas friends would have come north for an intervention.

Seven months into that pastorate, my father-in-law resigned the church in South Tulsa and asked if we would consider coming back to be the Lead Pastor. Although things had been going well for us in Oklahoma City, we allowed our name to be considered and ten days later we were voted in as pastor. At this time I moved my family back to Tulsa and we began what would become the fight of our lives.

To say it in compact form, my pastoring style was very different from my wife's dad. I had also discovered that as a pastor I was less adamant about the legalistic issues that were at the heart of the lifestyle identity of the denomination. The more I tried to fit in, the more I knew I didn't fit in anymore. By 2002, changes began to emerge in the culture of our church that reflected this reality.

In 2004, I called for a vote that would remove the church from the denominational affiliation—which in retrospect was a vote of confidence on myself as pastor. A vote against this would essentially be a vote against me, as pastor. After this night, I would know whether or not I needed to go somewhere else in pursuit of the vision God had placed in my heart. I resolved that if the church voted by desire to stay in denominational affiliation, I would resign as pastor. I explained my intent clearly to the eligible voters that night and they voted one hundred percent that we should go forward with disaffiliation.

Two weeks later another business meeting was held and an overwhelming majority voted to remove the church from affiliation with the denomination. I was surprised that there was only one dissenting vote that was cast that night and the rest were absolute in their affirmation for the direction at the previous business meeting. What I did not know at the time was that all of this would set in motion a chain reaction of events that I had not anticipated.

First, I had the full intent of retaining my ordination with the denomination, which would also keep the church in fellowship with the other churches in the denomination. This was my reality even though the officials with the denomination would later say to the contrary. I honestly felt that I would simply pastor on the liberal (less legalistic) side of the denomination and had no other plans at that point to do otherwise.

Most of my friends and family, most of my ministerial associations, and my beloved mentors were all in the denomination. I had no expectation or intention of breaking fellowship with all of these people at the time.

What I did not expect was the backlash that occurred immediately following the disaffiliation vote. Strong animosity rose up against us among those we considered friends and even family. There was no grace at all which was a fact that should not have surprised me. I was told that I simply needed to preach what I was being told was right even though I could not reconcile it with scripture. Many of the same people that had just voted their affirmation for change had fear set in as their family and friends from within the denomination began to cast a negative voice against us.

We were being accused as being deceived and even under a delusional spirit, sent by God, to damn us for eternity. I was also being attacked and alienated from the fellowship simply because my pastoral style was more tolerant than the other pastors that surrounded me in the region. It is true that I wasn't as strong when it came to enforcing the lifestyle codes propagated by the denomination. At the same time, I had not changed on the fundamentals of their doctrine at this time. People were turning against us and we really didn't know how all of this was going to turn out.

It was at this juncture that I realized my walk with God centered on self-works rather than on Grace Works. I realized that I had to do something about it. In a little more than three months after that fateful business meeting, I surrendered my ordination with the denomination and began the task of founding a new, non-denominational church.

Throughout this book I will give some details of our ministry experience before and after this departure. I want to give you an understanding of how I arrived at the Grace Life, doing Grace Works, and living for Kingdom Advance. One thing for sure, our departure from the denomination proved to be a catalyst for change that would bring me to this wonderful truth.

In the years that followed, many other wonderful things happened including having the opportunity to forge new fellowship with like-minded ministries, seeing a turnover of dedicated congregants that share in the vision God gave me as pastor, and having the opportunity to enroll in Oral Roberts University and completing my Master of Divinity degree in the School of Theology and Ministry. As it stands, all of these experiences—both of tragedy and triumph—brought knowledge concerning the Grace Life, Grace Works, and the wonderful opportunity for Kingdom Advance.

I realize that at this point in your reading you may be a bit confused by my terminology, so hang in there. The original question remains to be unraveled, and now I have introduced a new one, "What are Grace Works?" It is my attempt to take a little bit of your time to answer both questions. Hopefully the end result will be to bring life transformation to you! That is the purpose of this book. To set us all free from self-works and to see us rise up in the joy of living the Grace Life—all for the purpose of Kingdom Advance.

In order for it to take full hold, we must be liberated from all influences of legalism and find ourselves operating in the higher calling of the Grace Life. As we begin, we must first set our hearts to pray for the illumination of the Holy Spirit. After that, let's take some time and join together in this Grace Life journey! Ultimately we can all proclaim the good news that *GOD DID THAT!*

Chapter One

THE GRACE LIFE

In order to unpack the meaning of the Grace Life we must first look at the prevailing understanding of grace in the world of Christianity. As many already know, the predominate definition of grace in the modern world is, "The unmerited favor of God." I am not so arrogant to believe that this definition is wrong, everybody else has it incorrect, and I have been given some higher understanding. My intention here is not as much to define grace, as it is to expand the understanding of grace beyond this foundational definition.

Certainly, grace *is* the unmerited favor of God working on our behalf! I am not here to refute that. My only contention is that many times definitions like this fall short of giving us the full extent found in the context of a word. Grace understood only by the parameters of this popular definition does not reveal the full impact of how grace is operating in "present action" in someone's life. In order to live the Grace Life, we must understand grace in its fullest extent. This understanding not only sees grace on the linear level of the defined word, but also on the multi-dimensional level of a life defined by its impact.

It seems clear that the formal definition has its roots in an Old Testament Hebrew understanding of grace. For instance, in Genesis 6:8 the bible reveals that, "Noah found grace in the eyes of the Lord." The word *chen* is translated "grace" and is commonly defined as "favor" because this is the connotation in the original language. To be clear, this word is simply defined as "favor" and the implication is sure. Noah, in the Old Testament context, found the favor of God for salvation and by that favor he was instructed to build an ark of safety.

Where it differs from the expanded idea of grace is that the actual implementation of his salvation—the building of the ark—was wrought by his own abilities and strength. Noah labored for years under his own ability (and that of his sons) to build the ark of safety for his family in order to merit the salvation God was providing. As a fan of comedian Bill Cosby, I have often laughed at his skit about Noah. Mr. Cosby's attempt at humor reveals some level of truth for us concerning grace. In the skit, God instructs Noah to build the ark out of Gopher wood. Noah then asks God what Gopher wood is and God replies, "Shut up Noah and go for wood." There is no doubt that Noah had favor, but he still had to build the ark under his own power, strength, and ability. He had to go for wood and it was hard labor. God's instruction to build the ark and the human effort exercised by Noah and his sons combined to make a way of escape for them.

What needs to be clarified is that the writers of the New Testament clearly expanded the idea of grace in the church as going beyond favor. The predominate word used for "grace" is the Greek word, *charis*. James Strong makes the point that this is, "the divine influence upon the heart and its reflection in the life."[1] This grace also shares in its root the word *charisma*, which ultimately means the working of divine power (as in healing) and divine influence (as in appeal). There is further evidence in the New Testament writings that the understanding of grace incorporates at least three attributes from God: divine favor, divine influence, and divine power.

Grace in the New Testament context goes beyond a foundational understanding that stops with God's favor. Matter of fact, grace is favor and a whole lot more. In order to live the Grace Life, we must broaden our idea of grace to incorporate all three attributes of divine favor, influence, and power. We must then explore the various ways by which grace is applied to our life and how this grace reflects the work of God through us.

This is the essence of the Grace Life. We do not attempt to do Kingdom things on the merit of our own strength and ability. Instead, everything we do comes as a result of divine favor, influence, and power! This broadens the understanding of grace to incorporate the favor of God giving us the *opportunity*, the influence of God giving us the *strategy*, and the power of God giving us the *ability*. Grace takes on various forms as it works in us to accomplish Kingdom purpose. 1 Peter 4:10-11 gives us a launching point for this understanding.

> 1 Peter 4:10–11 (NIV84) — Each one should use whatever gift he has received to serve others, faithfully administering God's grace in its various forms. If anyone speaks, he should

do it as one speaking the very words of God. If anyone serves, he should do it with the strength God provides, so that in all things God may be praised through Jesus Christ. To him be the glory and the power for ever and ever. Amen.

Peter emphatically declares that we are to faithfully administer God's grace in its various forms. He did not indicate grace in a singular context. The implication here is clear that his idea of grace was expanded beyond favor since a reasonable assessment would find that the favor of God cannot be administered by individuals in the church. What a calamity that would be if the idea of grace in the New Testament church stopped at divine favor and then we were given the power to administer it. As I alluded to in my opening remarks, I have been involved with people in church life that would refrain from administering God's favor to me if given the opportunity. There have also been times when I probably would have withheld his favor from others as well. I have drawn from this the conclusion that grace must be more than divine favor in order for us to have the opportunity to administer it to one another.

Peter also declares in this passage that grace has in it various forms, not just one form. This is where the Grace Life takes shape! The Grace Life (living under divine favor, influence, and power) is producing in our lives Grace Works (operating under divine favor, influence, and power). These verses in 1 Peter 4 show that we have received grace gifts as a result of *divine favor*. He then declares that if we speak, the words should be as if the very words of God are being spoken.

That is *divine influence*! He continues by saying that if we serve, it should be done under the strength God provides. That is *divine power*!

Grace is divine favor, divine power, and divine influence. We now see that grace is the fuel behind everything accomplished in the Kingdom of God. It is not what we do on our own that makes a difference. It is what we do as a result of grace that counts! It is God's favor! It is God's strength! It is God's ability working through us. It is His desire that comes from His heart placed in our hearts! In turn, we are influenced to act upon it.

To put this into perspective let me give you an example. If you use the idea of New Testament grace in a salvation manner then grace is divine favor, influence, and power enabling someone to be saved. This is not by someone's own power but by the power of God! Every aspect of the process of salvation is initiated and conducted by the grace of God.

We need to move beyond the scope of salvation when discussing grace though. Let me put it bluntly that grace doesn't stop with salvation! Neither is grace only applied as the vehicle for salvation. Grace in its various forms is expanded to carry past initial conversion to become the source of power, strength, and ability in our lives for Christian maturity and productivity. This is clarified in Ephesians 2:4-10.

> Ephesians 2:4–10 (niv84) — But because of his great love for us, God, who is rich in mercy, made us alive with Christ even when we were dead in transgressions—it is by grace you have

been saved. And God raised us up with Christ and seated us with him in the heavenly realms in Christ Jesus, in order that in the coming ages he might show the incomparable riches of his grace, expressed in his kindness to us in Christ Jesus. For it is by grace you have been saved, through faith—and this not from yourselves, it is the gift of God—not by works, so that no one can boast. For we are God's workmanship, created in Christ Jesus to do good works, which God prepared in advance for us to do.

Paul instructs in this passage that by grace we are saved as a gift from God—not by our own works. In other words, you have not been saved by the merit of your own ability and strength. Paul then expands the idea of grace in the tenth verse—we have been created in Christ Jesus to do good works. This almost seemed like an oxymoron to me. How contradictory is it to say that it is not by works and then turn right around and say we are created to do good works? Is it works or is it not works? I needed to know the answer to that question.

You will stay confused about this if you do not understand the Grace Life. Grace and works are not polar opposites in contradiction to each other when we are living the Grace Life. The significant difference between the works mentioned in the ninth verse and those mentioned in the tenth is the *source* of those works. The first "works" are those we do on our own but the second "good works" are those that are done through divine favor, influence, and power—the Grace

Life! Grace caries past initial conversion and becomes the source of power, strength, and ability to do God's will as God's new workmanship creation.

I must clarify that just as it is with most things, grace has dangerous extremes associated with it. One way to describe these dangerous extremes is to consider the point that on each side of grace there is a ditch that we could fall into if we are not careful. To one side there is the ditch of legalistic grace. This is an out of balance view that pits grace against works. Those who fall into this ditch argue that there are no works associated with grace at all.

The other side has the ditch of legalistic works. Those who espouse legalistic works over emphasize works to a point that they become a prerequisite to grace. Works based legalism is ugly because it puts works ahead of grace in the Christian experience. It is a monster that is never satisfied because once in the ditch of legalistic self-works there are never enough things to do to earn God's favor. With this said, the true scriptural mandate concerning grace and works is balance. We land somewhere in the middle of these two ditches living the Grace Life and accomplishing Grace Works under the umbrella of divine favor, influence, and power.

Grace and works accompany each other in that it is impossible to do God's will without his favor, influence, and power as the driving force. Again let me emphasize, Grace and works are not pitted against each other, they work together to accomplish God's purpose—Kingdom Advance! When we get it wrong is when we have works without God's grace as the source or we have grace without works as the result. This is what makes legalism in either direction so toxic.

Works without grace are flesh driven instead of being Spirit led. Grace without good works brings Kingdom ineffectiveness and spiritual lethargy. Legalistic works create frustration on the part of the individual because *it is impossible to live for God without God*! Legalistic grace creates frustration because *it is impossible to live for God without working for God.* The good news is that we can live for God productively when resting in the truth found in the Grace Life. *God did that.*

Chapter Two

FALLING AWAY FROM GRACE

Falling away from grace is certainly not the most positive or joyful title one could put on a chapter but then again, it is a subject we must address if we are going to live the Grace Life. I have struggled through the years trying to understand what falling away from grace actually means. In my past experience it meant, "backsliding." In simplistic terms, that simply meant to slide back into the former sinful lifestyle and mentality thus canceling out the redemptive work of Christ in one's life.

This would mean a repositioning into the state of being lost again and revoking the benefits of salvation. In the theological framework of a legalistic religion falling away was easy. It was really easy. A person would be considered backslide simply by being involved with a forbidden activity such as going to the movie theater, to the bowling ally, or by wearing a forbidden article of clothing. Catch that! You could literally fall away from grace by the outfit you chose for the day or the wrong choice of recreational fun.

Others see falling away into a backslide state as a complete return to a lifestyle that is contrary to the will of God. This falling away is more tied to the works of the flesh listed in Galatians chapter five than a denominations code of rules and regulations of control. While appreciating the theological stand that states as a matter of human will a person can walk away from their salvation experience, one can also believe that the grace of God is big enough to sustain us through our human weaknesses, failures, and theological misunderstandings.

One does not have to espouse what many call a "once saved always saved" eternal security theology in order to believe, "Once saved not so easy to be lost." When living the Grace Life, you do not have to live in fear of falling away and being lost, especially since everyone who is in Christ is eternally secure. I do not believe that we should live in fear of a weak, shaky salvation experience. We should not live our Christian experience constantly afraid that our salvation can be ripped from us at every turn. It is true that because of the sinful nature, we are all subject to an ongoing fight between good and evil in us. Sometimes we make mistakes and even commit sinful acts, which we know are contrary to the will of God in our lives. The sigh of relief is that God knows our heart and because of His favor, influence, and power we are not cast away even when we fail.

It seemed necessary to establish this point so that the remaining portion of this chapter would not direct us towards questioning the work of grace in our lives in the sense of salvation. God's plan and desire for us is that we have confidence and a strong sense of security in the salvation that has been given to us. One of the problematic mentalities that works-based legalism creates is that it does not allow for that sense of security. When someone thinks that salvation is earned by personal merit based on works, then it is hard to be secure. The natural progression is that if performance saves then performance damns. You can literally fall away from salvation at any moment simply by making a mistake or by doing something wrong.

I pastored a church in Oklahoma City in 1998 that had been subjected to several decades of legalistic works theology. The people in that congregation were in constant fear that at any minute a simple mistake could rip any hope of an eternity with God from them. Falling away from grace was easy in their estimation. The pastor prior to our time as pastor was very hard concerning the various issues of lifestyle identity propagated by the denomination. One of those issues was a "no tolerance" stand against television. In order to be a functioning member in that denomination you were forbidden to own a television.

I understand that for many readers this seems preposterous and you would like a further explanation. Please continue without one seeing I really don't want to waste any more time on the intricate details of such legalistic religious regulations imposed by certain denominations. Let it suffice to say that some pastors, including this one, took this rule that forbade television ownership to the extreme and forbid the people in the church from ever watching a television at the risk of being lost. They were warned that God was so against T.V. that a simple glance at one would damn them eternally to Hell.

This was illustrated in detail to me on a trip to a store shortly after assuming the pastorate. This particular store was one of the big box stores with an electronics section. They had a row of televisions, all of which were tuned into a station in order to show their picture quality. I was standing down the aisle and noticed a mother from our new church and her teenage kids walking towards me. As they approached the electronics section they all raised their hand to shield their eyes from the televisions that were on their right. Every one of them did this at the same moment. They were so afraid of losing their salvation, or falling away, over television that they could not take the chance at any temptation to glance that direction!

To them, falling away from grace meant that the grace of God working in their life was not enough to keep them saved in the electronics section of a local store. This cannot be what falling away from grace actually means. Experiences such as this led me to begin a quest to find out what falling away from grace really does mean. In this context, we must turn to Paul's words concerning this in Galatians 5:4.

> Galatians 5:4 (NIV84)—You who are trying to be justified by law have been alienated from Christ; you have fallen away from grace.

Paul clearly ties the result of falling away from grace to the act of attempting to find justification by obeying the old law. In other words, instead of believing that personal justification comes as a result of grace, one falls back into a mindset that our own works and obedience to lifestyle rules and regulations are what justify us. Falling away from grace is to fall from the position of being justified by God's favor, influence, and power and back into a mindset of being justified by our own efforts and means.

It seems plausible that some people in the early church had gotten a hold of the idea that they could go back to being justified in the eyes of God through human effort and ability. They had slipped back, or fallen away, into a "law" relationship with God. So now, instead of their justification coming as a result of divine favor, influence, and power, they felt it came as a result of obeying law and doing certain things.

With this as context, to fall away from grace means to no longer be influenced by divine leading and conviction but now law, rules, and restrictions are the driving force behind what we are doing. It seems likely to me that those legalistic pastors had more in common with falling away from grace than the people who would glance at or own a television. It is clear that to Paul falling away from grace had to do with returning to a rules led religion and away from a Spirit led relationship with God.

Many people try to live their Christian life under their own strength and ability. In pastoring, I have found that many times people get frustrated because of the constant effort to do this thing on their own. It is frustrating! We have a divine edict to advance the Kingdom and then try to advance it with our own effort, ability, and strength. It is a mundane experience to be handed the list of rules and obligations and then get a pat on the back from the preacher with a "good luck" and "go get 'em tiger." It makes no sense!

We walk into this Christian life knowing that we can't save ourselves yet then set out to try to accomplish Kingdom life on our own. Too many Christians find it a struggle to discover balance in this because it is true that anyone can obey a list of rules and regulations in a religious sense. Anyone can muster up the self-fortitude to do what needs to be done. With tight grips and white knuckles people are working themselves into a state of weariness, all in the attempt to do what they think is God's bidding. It should be clear that trying to live and work for God on our own only leads to discouragement and legalistic self-righteousness. The ultimate price of this self-works lifestyle is unhappiness and even bitterness.

Going back to the television example, anyone can make a decision to not own or watch a television. Anyone can see a list of rules and do what is written. If, "Don't watch T.V." is on the list, then don't watch T.V. It's that simple. An attitude then emerges that since you are now in obedience to the rule, God's favor is on you and you are saved. The problem is that religion without relationship is restriction and frustration ensues. The by-product of this is fear that any breach of the rules means automatic divine disapproval and a loss of eternal security.

The frustration is compounded by the fact that many of these rules are the institute of man and not the intent of God. Was God really waiting with his finger on the disapproval button in the lives of that single mom and her teenage children as they walked in that store? I detest the idea that our God would be that cruel. These precious people were living in fear in the name of God, as unbelievable as it seems. This incident was another piece of the puzzle that changed my way of thinking. I realized what they (and I) had been taught could not be grace.

Under grace you don't have to establish a rule such as "no television." As we all know, there are good and bad things aired on the various television offerings. Some things on television should be avoided simply because of what they portray and the kind of desires they incite in the mind and spirit of the individual. Surely I don't have to clarify that any further. At the same time, there are many things on television that bring no harm at all and are even helpful and inspirational. This is an issue of Holy Spirit led control and not an issue of complete abstinence.

The same can be said about several other things considered taboos in certain sectors of the Western church. Many good people have been turned away from the church because of a judgmental abstinence stand on such things as tattoos, body piercings, hairstyles, and the moderate consumption of alcohol. Obviously, there are many views in Western Christian circles concerning things like these, ranging from complete intolerance to full liberality. I want to be clear that it is not my intent or purpose in this text to be an opponent or advocate of what would be considered controversial subjects among so many.

My earnest desire is to simply bring into consideration the idea that Spirit led control and religious tolerance in many areas are far more advantageous than people being bound by rules, cultures, and traditions that are not truly supported by the scripture. Scriptural guidelines and Holy Spirit influence are far more productive than man-made standards, religious manipulation, cultural conditioning, and fear. Our responsibility is to divide the word of God in a right way—never reading into the text what is not there. We also must be careful not to make personal preferences, or even personal weaknesses, contentious points of absolute doctrine.

Being responsible to the text, we understand that there are many areas where the scripture does promote abstinence. In these areas, we abstain. These areas include sexual immorality, jealousy, getting drunk, stealing, lying, murder, hatred, and gossiping. The Holy Spirit will *never* lead you to violate God's moral character in areas such as these. But in the areas where scripture speaks of moderation, or doesn't speak at all, we must be careful to steer clear of setting legalistic rules in a response to tradition, culture, personal weakness, or religious intolerance.

When I was a teenager there was a man who taught one of the Sunday school classes I attended. This man would eventually go on to pastor a church. He wondered into this Pentecostal church in the late 1970s and had a radical conversion from the life he was living. To give you some background, this man was the epitome of an American southern country boy—some would say he was a "redneck." His hair was cut extremely short with a greased combed back style, he always wore blue jeans and boots, and he was actively involved with beer joints and bar fights.

Keep in mind that this was his lifestyle in the 1960s and 1970s. The culture for youth in America during this time was predominately influenced by the hippie revolution and the disco age. Needless to say, the "redneck" country crowd despised the hippies and disco crowd to the point of making sport out of tracking them down on the streets and beating them with fists and ball bats. This man's pre-Christ pastime was to slide on his blue jeans, go have a few beers, and then go find some hippies to hit. Then came Christ and all of this changed for him. As you can imagine, he immediately felt impressed to stop doing these things.

I told you this to give you a picture of the reasons for what would transpire in his life. Soon after conversion this man was getting dressed for the day and began to put on his favorite pair of jeans. While doing that, he felt the old feeling of bar room escapades and hippie bashing that he remembered from days gone by. Those blue jeans represented and reminded him of something in his past that was dark and ugly. At that, he made a vow to God that he would never wear a pair of blue jeans again.

Here was a personal preference boundary that was rooted in what these items of clothing represented to him. I have no problem with that! What happened after that is the problem. This man took his personal preference and began to declare that blue jeans were wrong in the eyes of God for everyone. As he taught us in the classroom, he would make comments about the evils of wearing blue jeans and the spirit of rebellion that was in them. He even took some verses out of context to support his new "blue jean" theology. As I watched him move further into ministry, he took this anti-blue jean doctrine into pastoring and imposed it upon the members of the congregation.

What he failed to understand was that very few people share in his background. What blue jeans represented to him did not apply to most people. This man had a weakness that was conditioned by his culture and would have been better off to practice abstinence personally while offering liberty to those who did not share in his circumstance. You cannot make a doctrine out of personal preferences and expect the word of God to back you up when it doesn't.

When you truly live the Grace Life, the Holy Spirit gives you the guidelines that are necessary for your own walk with God in the realm of moderation and tolerance. If your personal background and dependency issues need abstinence, grace will lead you there, even if others have liberty in the same area. For them, it may be an issue of moderation or complete liberty and not abstinence. In fact, grace allows for individual parameters in the areas where the scripture establishes liberty or moderation. The grace of God determines what is wholesome and productive for personal spiritual wellbeing and will place a check in your spirit when something is not.

One must also understand that what may be a hindrance to one person may not be to another. Here is where we get it wrong! You should never make a church wide doctrine out of your personal devotion. It is important to keep a healthy balance between personal liberty and personal devotion while not falling into the trap of being judgmental in either parameter. It is also important to note that we should never fall into the pit of feeling that our devotions make us more holy or righteous than others.

On the other hand, we must be very careful not to flaunt our liberties in the face of those who may not understand them. I am of the opinion that this is more about attitude than the particular action. Those attitudes must stand the test of Christian character. In 1 Corinthians 8:9 Paul called the kinds of people who would not understand our liberty in certain areas, "Weak." There is a Christian responsibility to protect the weak in light of those who are stronger. Study this verse with an open heart.

> 1 Corinthians 8:9 (NIV84)—Be careful, however, that the exercise of your freedom does not become a stumbling block to the weak.

The issue in this address by Paul was concerning those in the church that had no negative feelings concerning liberty in eating meat offered to idols. Obviously to these people it was a non-issue. Paul even admits that in God's eyes the eating of this meat doesn't make them better or worse. To Paul, God was also neutral on this subject. While at the same time there were others who would not understand this liberty and it would become a source for failing in their Christian confession.

Paul instructed those who felt liberty to be careful in their liberty so that it would not be a stumbling block to those who were weaker in their confession of faith.

He even went as far in the seriousness of this discourse to declare that if what he ate caused someone to fall into sin, he would not only refrain from eating the meat offered to idols, he would never eat any type of meat again.

There is no evidence that Paul or the Corinthian Christians ever went to this extreme, but the point was clear that for the sake of Christian unity and encouragement we should be mindful of our actions in front of those who would not understand. In the Grace Life we understand this principle and are influenced by the Holy Spirit to balance our devotions and liberties to live as an encourager and not as a discourager.

In the corporate sense, when we make rules outside of scriptural mandates we are walking towards law instead of grace. I am not saying rules are wrong per se, I am saying that no amount of rules obedience earns freedom, favor, and salvation. I am also saying that when rules replace relationship something is out of balance. Any rule in the corporate setting should be firmly established in scriptural mandates and not established from any other source.

I want it to be clear that what I am calling "rules" are lifestyle parameters that scripture establishes for productive and healthy boundaries. On a personal sense, the boundaries can also be non-scriptural mandates that vary from person to person. In either sense, corporate or personal, everything should be done under grace and not under law. Blindly obeying rules because that is what the denomination or preacher said is not what the Grace Life is all about.

This falls directly in line with why we need the Grace Life to begin with. In the Grace Life, we are not blindly obeying the rules and regulations of religious order and self-accomplishments. We are in fact following the leading of the Holy Spirit to walk in His will for us as an individual in everything we do. What we do should be Grace Works. The difference between law works and Grace Works is staggering. Works done under law are what we do on our own without divine favor, influence, and power while good works done under grace are the works done as a result of divine favor, influence, and power.

We avoid certain things not because the rules say to avoid them but because the Spirit is leading us to avoid them. This happens either by personal devotion or by illumination of a scriptural precept. On the other side, when we try to justify ourselves by our own effort we alienate ourselves from Christ. The redemptive work wrought by Christ on Calvary as been made of no effect in us because the cross is voided by human ability to act. Who needs His work when we can do this thing on our own?

I have attempted to establish the point that the Grace Life is a higher way to live. I must state emphatically that grace, not rules, must be the fuel behind everything we do—even when what we do is good. Paul made this declaration in Romans 11:6.

> Romans 11:6 (NIV84)—And if by grace, then it is no longer by works; if it were, grace would no longer be grace.

The Grace Life is to understand that it is not what we do on our own that makes the difference. It begins with the favor Christ purchased for us on Calvary and flows down into what he is now doing through us. These are the works that matter! If it were contingent on our works then grace would no longer be grace. That is a powerful statement to say the least.

One thing we should note is that in the Grace life there is still "doing." The difference is that the source of that doing is vastly different than that of self-works! In the Grace Life we "do" because of what God has done and is doing in and through us. Our actions are then sourced by God and not by or own inventions and intentions. There must be a clear distinction made in this or we lose focus on what needs to happen.

Grace Works are those things done by grace—divine favor, influence, and power. If what we do originates from anywhere else, we have bypassed grace and are now operating in fleshly law works. Grace is no longer grace when it comes to our actions and we have fallen away from grace back into law. As we will examine at length in a little bit, *God did that so that I can do this!*

Chapter Three

GRACE MAKES US FREE

The monkey is off our back! I don't know if that particular saying means the same thing to everyone that it meant to us in my East Texas upbringing, but to us it simply meant that we are off the hook and no longer responsible! That is a message of freedom. So many times people come into a Christian walk, feel the effects of freedom that faith brings, but then step back into a sense of bondage to religious systems and legalistic lifestyles. It's as though the monkey of sin and godlessness is off our back but then the monkey of personal obligation and self-works crawls up there in its place.

Whether we want to admit it or not, people tend to fall back into a mentality that they have to do this or that in order to keep themselves safe from eternal damnation and in the center of God's favor. As examined in the previous chapter, our justification comes as a work of God's grace and the redemption purchased by Christ and not as a result of our own works. We cannot earn justification through self-works. This is clearly stated in Titus 3:7-8.

> Titus 3:7–8 (NIV84)—so that, having been justified by his grace, we might become heirs having the hope of eternal life. This is a trustworthy saying. And I want you to stress these things, so that those who have trusted in God may be careful to devote themselves to doing what is good. These things are excellent and profitable for everyone.

There is no question that our justification comes by his grace and through him we are heirs of eternal life. This word, "justified" comes from the original Greek word, "dikaiŏŏ" which means to render (that is, *show* or *regard* as) just or innocent.[2] This is only one of many New Testament verses that declare we are made just or innocent, not by the merit of our own works, but by the grace of God. We are truly set free by divine favor, divine influence, and divine power! Grace has set us free from the condemnation wrought by our sinful nature.

The important thing to remember about the Grace Life is that we are also set free from the obligation of law. God set law in place as a means of justification until He sent his Son, Jesus Christ, into the world to settle the issue of sin once and for all. God's law covenant with the people in the Old Testament set up a system of rules and regulations that the people were then obligated to follow. They offered sacrifices, they obeyed dietary and lifestyles restrictions, and they observed feast and Sabbath days. They also circumcised their male children as a sign of obedience. These things were the human conditions to the covenant of law. God accepted these practices, along with many other categories of regulated actions, as enough to cover their transgressions for a time.

Under this paradigm, as long as the people fulfilled the obligation of law in their lives they walked in the favor and blessing of God. Law came with a clear list of blessings for obedience and curses for disobedience. The difficulty here is that they were on their own for the most part in fulfilling these obligations. As a result of their own inability to perform, we find their many failures recorded in the Old and New Testaments. Over and over again the people found themselves transgressing the obligations of the law and then reaping the consequences of their actions.

One of the problems in the church today is that many people are trying to live in the New Testament church under an Old Testament paradigm. We must settle the issue once and for all that grace sets us free from the obligation of personal performance as found in the Old Testament law covenant. No longer do we have to fulfill lifestyle requirements to merit the favor and blessing of God. We are free from the obligation of works as a means of earning from God that which we need to survive and thrive.

This does not mean that we can abuse the work of grace in our lives. Some have taken the idea of freedom under grace and used it as an excuse to live however they want to in unrestrained behavior. Grace does not set us free in order that we can continue being a slave to the sinful nature and its fruit. Far from that! This very issue was dealt with in Romans 6:12-18.

Romans 6:12–18 (NIV84)—Therefore do not let sin reign in your mortal body so that you obey its evil desires. Do not offer the parts of your body to sin, as instruments of wickedness, but rather offer yourselves to God, as those who have been brought from death to life; and offer the parts of your body to him as instruments of righteousness. For sin shall not be your master, because you are not under law, but under grace. What then? Shall we sin because we are not under law but under grace? By no means! Don't you know that when you offer yourselves to someone to obey him as slaves, you are slaves to the one whom you obey—whether you are slaves to sin, which leads to death, or to obedience, which leads to righteousness? But thanks be to God that, though you used to be slaves to sin, you wholeheartedly obeyed the form of teaching to which you were entrusted. You have been set free from sin and have become slaves to righteousness.

Throughout the history of the church people have tried to excuse all kinds of evil behavior by pulling the grace card. They say that their actions don't matter because they are not under law but under grace. There is a clear understanding given in these verses that living under grace is not a license to participate in sinful behavior. The truth of the matter is that if you are living under grace you will be led to pursue righteous behavior as a result of divine influence. The writer here is making a bold declaration that as the people of God we should not willingly offer our bodies to sinful practices using grace to excuse it.

At the same time, we must beware because it is at this point that legalism tries to set itself up! Some fall into the trap of believing that since there are certain actions that are against God's moral and righteous nature and are viewed by him as sin, there must be a list of rules we need to follow in order to stay on the straight and narrow. Their point evolves to a notion that any deviation from that list removes the individual from God's grace and they must then amend their actions to earn God's favor again. The point needs to be made that it is not a list of rules that we need to follow but the influence of the Holy Spirit through grace. Paul dealt with this in Galatians 5:19-25.

> Galatians 5:19–25 (NIV84)—The acts of the sinful nature are obvious: sexual immorality, impurity and debauchery; idolatry and witchcraft; hatred, discord, jealousy, fits of rage, selfish ambition, dissensions, factions and envy; drunkenness, orgies, and the like. I warn you, as I did before, that those who live like this will not inherit the kingdom of God. But the fruit of the Spirit is love, joy, peace, patience, kindness, goodness, faithfulness, gentleness and self-control. Against such things there is no law. Those who belong to Christ Jesus have crucified the sinful nature with its passions and desires. Since we live by the Spirit, let us keep in step with the Spirit.

He first lists particular actions that are born in the sinful nature and would constitute sinful practices in God's eyes. He then goes on to say that these things inhibit or even prohibit ownership of the Kingdom of God in our lives. How can there be Kingdom Advance if there are Kingdom inhibitors in us? At this point we must decide how we solve this dilemma in the context of grace and not law.

First, we must discover what it means to obey in the context of the Grace Life. Two simple words solve the issue of obedience—*faith* and *action*. Our faith in the gospel and the work of Jesus Christ is enough to save us. We must then understand that the actions—Grace Works—that are being produced in our lives should be Spirit led and not flesh driven. This is the key to overcoming the acts of the sinful nature. It is not to get a list of rules and white knuckle obey them, it is allowing the Holy Spirit to influence and empower our actions to do his will and to overcome the acts of the sinful nature.

Grace has set us free from the way of life that tries to gain righteousness by human effort and flesh driven works. The Grace Life has set us free to bear the fruit of the Spirit in our lives that produces the kind of actions that are pleasing to God. The Fruit of the Spirit is the *only* antidote for the acts of the sinful nature (or the works of the flesh). The Fruit of the Spirit produces both moderation and abstinence and gives us the power to be effective in the Kingdom.

We crucified the sinful nature by faith when we believed in our heart that God raised Christ from the dead and confessed with our mouth that Jesus is Lord according to Romans 10:8-13. The ultimate victory of this faith confession is that we continue on in our Christian journey being led by the Holy Spirit. If every action has a subsequent reaction then we must believe that the act of grace in our lives produces righteous actions on our part as we grow in faith and knowledge.

This is important to remember! Living the Grace Life means that we have been set free from the bondage to sin and that we have willfully (by faith) given ourselves to God as "slaves" to divine favor, influence, and power. This gives us the opportunity to "devote ourselves to doing what is good"—going back to Titus 3:8. Not as a means of earning salvation and favor but a natural outflow of the salvation and favor that has been given to us by faith.

Now that we have been set free from the obligation of law, we can concentrate on what the Holy Sprit is doing through us in our attitudes and actions. This is not about what we are doing per se but about what the Holy Spirit is doing in and through us. These actions are not the result of our own ability and strength to follow the rules; they are the result of divine favor, influence, and power. Grace makes us free!

This also liberates us from the tyranny of preachers and denominations with super egos and manipulative control over the people. Some of the worst products of legalism are ministers who rule with an iron fist and use the twisting of God's word as a means to control people through fear and manipulation. Firmly establish in your heart that grace influences through love and blessing and never manipulates through fear. Our God of grace is not in the fear business. This is clearly demonstrated in Romans 8:15.

> Romans 8:15 (niv84)—For you did not receive a spirit that makes you a slave again to fear, but you received the Spirit of sonship. And by him we cry, "Abba, Father."

What a thought! We are sons, not slaves to fear! As a child of God we can have full assurance of his love and care for us and do not have to live in fear. Some time ago I preached in the exact opposite of this thought environment at a church on the East Coast of the Unites States. Thankfully, I was passing through New Jersey and would only have to deal with this church and pastor on a single Sunday. I have rarely seen anything like it as far as a fearful church environment is concerned.

I should have known something was up by the large black guard dogs that were chained to the porch of the church as we walked in. These dogs were chained in such a way as to come together towards the middle of the porch with low growls and snarling teeth, just out of reach of those entering the church foyer. I hope you can get the picture here. The pastor stood back and watched in amusement at the reaction of the people to his pets on the porch. He trained them to be as mean as vipers are in a corner—as mean as he was, I would soon find out.

This was all a game of fear and manipulation to him. The poor people that occupied the pews of that church lived under the shadow of a tyrant. Somehow, in their quest for God, they landed in his church and under his pastorate. He convinced them through his very strong and intimidating personality that God was with him and they had better not cross him or God would send judgment. These people had become slaves to fear.

During worship, this pastor sat on the platform glaring at the people—much like the two dogs on the porch. I would almost bet that if you could get close enough to him he'd be growling with a low-pitched snarl. Under this incessant scrutiny you could see the people struggling in their worship. I would soon find out that it wasn't as much God on their mind as it was fear that this pastor would not be pleased with their response to the music and songs. I don't know if he was trying to impress me or if he just went off every service, but he went off.

I watched as he grabbed the microphone from the hand of the song leader and screamed at the people that they had not clapped hard enough, they had not sung loud enough, and their worship was not demonstrative enough. He then yelled something to the effect that they had better get it right this time and ordered the song to be sung again. At that, he returned to his seat to continue his glaring observance. I tried to love on the people that day and was happy to see this place fade away into my rearview mirror. I never went back.

I have thought about that place many times. Christianity to these people was a dungeon of manipulation where they were slaves to fear. I have seen it more than once, and I know for a fact that legalism, fear, and manipulation are enemies of the Grace Life. This type of legalistic control doesn't even give the people an opportunity for the Grace Life. People who rely so much on the control of man with the rules and regulations of religious lifestyles find it very difficult to follow the divine influence of grace in operation.

I've even heard preachers make statements that amounted to them declaring themselves as the voice of God—even though what they were saying was clearly from their own spirit. As a point of clarification, I am not talking about someone being used by the gifts of the Spirit. There is a huge difference between being edified by a word of knowledge and being manipulated by the word of man. If you smell fear and manipulation, it is not the Grace Life for sure. Grace makes us free, it does not make us slaves to fear. Jesus gave us the tremendous promise of freedom in John 8:36.

> John 8:36 (NIV84)—So if the Son sets you free, you will be free indeed.

In Christ we are not just free—we are really free! That is a promise of blessing to hold on to. I experienced a similar situation in my own life to the one experienced by those poor people in New Jersey. Back in 1989, I pulled into Hammond, Louisiana thinking I was there to preach a weekend revival meeting. What I did not know was that the pastor of the church from which the invitation came had a much different agenda.

As a young man, I began an intenerate ministry as a traveling preacher in 1987. During the formative years, my preaching schedule was somewhat sporadic due to the fact that few pastors knew me and I had to build this ministry from scratch. By 1989, I was experiencing a regular preaching schedule, but I was very excited about this new opportunity and was hoping it would be a catalyst for other preaching contacts and engagements in Louisiana.

I know now that the pastor of the church in Hammond was much like the one described in the New Jersey story. He too had a ferocious, black watchdog that he had trained to be mean on command. He also had a very charismatic but demanding spirit and was very proficient at persuasive words and the craft of manipulation. I ended up not preaching for him that weekend but he encouraged me to stay and help out around the church. Because I didn't have anywhere else to go for a few weeks, I stayed and occupied myself by helping out there. Before I knew it, about four weeks had gone by.

As the days progressed this pastor became very possessive of me. He began to express to me that he no longer wanted me to travel out and preach at other churches. He almost had me convinced to move to Hammond to be his assistant. After several more weeks went by, I went to preach a meeting elsewhere and also had plans to go home to visit my family and friends in Houston. I will never forget how uncomfortable he acted about me leaving and made me aware of the fact that he was against it.

What was even more unusual was that he informed me that he wanted me back on a particular day. He was doing everything he could to stay in control of my life. As life would have it, I made the "mistake" of not returning to Hammond on this man's schedule. I will never forget how angry he became with me. He began to rant like a mad man. Because I had been away from his brainwashing type influence for a couple of weeks, I knew something was terribly wrong. After consulting with my family and my pastor, I made the decision to not return except to go back to get the possessions and clothes that I had left there. I made this return trip with the help and companionship of my older sister Amy.

Looking back it is almost humorous how she tried in vain to help me escape this place in a stealth kind of way on a Monday afternoon. We successfully snuck in but then got caught removing my possessions. We found out later that he had people from the church keeping watch in case I tried something like this. Amy and I ended up being surrounded, cornered to say the least, and I was threatened to be there that Wednesday evening for a "going away" event.

He then promised me that I would be able to leave with his "blessing" and with the rest of my stuff if I would come to it. Under fear for my safety and the safety of my belongings that were still at the church, which included a keyboard and amplifier, I agreed to show up for the Wednesday night event. This going away service turned out to be a "stand on the porch of the church and proclaim curses over me" event. Thankfully, I had left my sister with some friends in McComb, Mississippi so she didn't have to endure the wrath to come and the vile things that were said about her youngest sibling as he was trying to escape an insane situation.

I haven't shared this story often but I think it is important to the subject at hand. I could have been paralyzed by the words this man spoke over me—words of destruction and failure. His declaration was that God would destroy me because I was leaving his ministry oversight. These words echoed off of the cars on the gravel parking lot as I was walking away for good. I could have believed his legalistic curses and been paralyzed by fear but chose to let them fall to the ground.

Legalism has a way of encasing you with a sprit of fear. It is fueled by fear and manipulation and grace has no part in that. I drove out of that place determined to live above the curse—and I did! The ministry doors opened for me in a fantastic way after this experience, and I have never looked back. Since that time I have also discovered the Grace Life and have lived in God's favor and blessing in an abundant way. I refuse to be a slave to fear! Never forget that the Grace Life gives no place for manipulation and fear. When following grace, you will not be manipulated into doing something that the Holy Spirit has not influenced you or given you the power to do.

Throughout the years I have seen many people who were bound by the chains of negative words and hurtful deeds done to them. Matter of fact, their entire future is sabotaged by these negative words and events. They find themselves paralyzed in a state of hopelessness, discouragement, and fear. One thing that I have discovered is that just because someone says something doesn't mean it's true. I have also found that I am not responsible for how someone treats me but I am responsible for my reactions to it. I made up my mind to allow grace to shape my response even though I may not have understood the full implication of grace at the time. Grace declares a blessing that overrides the curse! Grace declares that no matter what was done, God is greater. People or circumstances cannot stop the Grace Life blessing.

The same held true some years later when I made the ministry decision to leave the denomination that I was raised in. As you may remember, in November of 1998, I assumed the Lead Pastor position at a church in South Tulsa that had been pastored by my father-in-law for more than twenty-eight years. I knew that certain issues would arise that would make this journey more difficult. To begin with, I had assisted him for almost three years and knew that we had some differences in style and theology. Even with these differences I felt that taking the assignment was the right thing to do, so I took it with faith in my heart. The environment of the church began to shift around 2002 and culminated in 2004 with the surrendering of my ordination with the denomination and launching a new non-denominational church.

I never actually expected things to go the way they did. As stated in the introduction, I honestly thought that although I would be considered on the liberal fringe of the denomination, I would still remain a part of the fellowship as an ordained minister. There were plenty of other examples in the denomination of this, so I felt in my mind that I was secure and that my leaving the denomination was a non-negotiable at least for the foreseeable future.

Reality showed in a matter of weeks that my place was not secure at all. I did not have the right location or the right personality to go against the grain like the others did in the denomination. They were not in Oklahoma, and I was. They were also big enough personalities in the denomination to do what they wanted to do without real repercussion—many of them with a ministry legacy wrapped up in their last name. On the other hand, I was the son of a non-preacher and my name and influence wasn't big enough to go against the expected tide.

Words fail to express how hard this was for my wife and me. I was simply trying to follow what I felt God was doing in my life, and my peers in the denomination could not have disagreed any more. In a few short weeks, we lost most of our friends and ministry affiliates. We also had family members turn their backs on us, which was really painful. There was a lot of animosity from people surrounding our decision to follow God's plan. We found that the church would need to re-launch because transition was not going to happen.

I was troubled by this reality as well. To be honest, no one wants his epitaph to read, "Here lays the man who closed the church his father-in-law pastored for twenty eight years." At this point, many negative things were said about us. Words such as deceiver, apostate, under a spirit of delusion, and lost were associated with our decision to leave the denomination. We even had people praying that we would fail. Then rumors and attacks against us personally started circulating. These rumors escalated to the point that they were saying that I had resigned the church and a mega-church had taken over our property and even that Raylene and I were divorced.

The great news is that God has the last say! False prayers and rumors like that are not the determining factors in our lives. Raylene and I weathered a very dark storm to come out on the winning team. Time progressed and we have been able to establish a church that encompasses the vision that God placed in our hearts for ministry that is centered on the Grace Life. The church we pastor has grown as a new congregation of happy and blessed people.

All of the evil spoken has been erased by the plan and will of God taking shape through surrendered lives and fleshed out through weekly ministry in a thriving congregation. I relate this to you to explain that although there may be people who do not understand the decisions you make or the paths you take, living the Grace Life is still living the best life possible. Anything that is said over you that is contrary to God's blessing must not be allowed to take root in your heart and mind. God has the last say; people and situations don't!

Grace makes us free from guilt, condemnation, manipulation, and fear. Grace takes us out from under the curses that have been pronounced over us. You will amount to something! You are beautiful! You can do it!

You are smart and strong! Things like this are what the Grace Life is pronouncing over you. Living under divine favor, influence, and power gives you the opportunity to be everything God has designed you to be and to do everything God has designed you to do. Grace makes us free. Never again do we have to cower down in doubt and despair with feelings of unworthiness and shame. Go for it! Refuse to be a slave to fear. You have been set free for Kingdom Advance! *God did that so that I can do this!*

Chapter Four

GRACE MAKES US FORCEFUL

"You really need to go to the Philippines with us!" These were the words my dear friend, Scott Presley, from Branson, Missouri said to me every time he invited me to join him on a mission trip to the Philippines. His prodding continued until I finally agreed to go in January 2010.

Harvest House International Ministries Philippines is a special place to say the least. Nestled on the Island of Mindanao, Harvest House is an oasis of God's love and power in a spiritually thirsty part of the world. After multiple trips there, I can truly say that my life and ministry are more blessed as a result of Kingdom involvement with them.

It was at a Harvest House crusade in Davao City that I first heard the words, "Kingdom Advance" used in the context I am referring to in this book. It resonated deep in my spirit as my faith was reinforced by a fresh presentation of the idea that God is interested in us being forceful participants in Kingdom Advance right now! It isn't as though I didn't know that. I have been preaching faith and spiritual renewal for decades. But this particular way of expressing it gave new life to an old message. My desire for Kingdom Advance had a fresh zeal to it.

Since I have been throwing this terminology around for a while let me give you some context to go by. This idea of Kingdom Advance and forceful participants comes from the niv84 translation of Matthew 11:12.

> Matthew 11:12 (niv84)—From the days of John the Baptist until now, the kingdom of heaven has been forcefully advancing, and forceful men lay hold of it.

In my opinion, this is the most accurate translation of this verse. The arrival of Jesus Christ in ministry forcefully advanced the Kingdom of God. It is also true that his plan is for forceful people to become participants in this advancing Kingdom. The Grace Life embodies this concept. Kingdom Advance is the agenda of God on the Earth and divine favor, divine influence, and divine power give us the ability and desire to take part in it. The Grace life is the life of forceful people who are Kingdom Advancers.

It is in this context that we find grace taking on several attributes that produce Kingdom forcefulness in our lives. It is also in this realm that we find grace taking on the various forms mentioned in 1 Peter 4:10. At the heart of this divine force is the reality that grace is our *enabler*.

The church has never been expected to perform the task of advancing the Kingdom of God on its own. The honest truth is that we are not able to do this on our own, even if we wanted to! The work we do is not by our own ability and strength but by the grace of God. This is the revelation found in 1 Corinthians 15:10.

> 1 Corinthians 15:10 (NIV84)—But by the grace of God I am what I am, and his grace to me was not without effect. No, I worked harder than all of them—yet not I, but the grace of God that was with me.

Paul recognized that everything he was doing was the result of grace and not the result of his own ability. Grace enabled him to be who he was and gave him the power to do what he was doing. With this in mind one could say that it is through divine favor, influence, and power that we are what we are. Divine favor, influence, and power have worked by grace and enabled us to work harder than anyone else.

We are forceful because grace enables us to be forceful. It is not law that makes the difference. Rules are not the driving force behind our effectiveness. Grace is! Divine favor, influence and power! This is also addressed in 2 Corinthians 1:12.

> 2 Corinthians 1:12 (NIV84)—Now this is our boast: Our conscience testifies that we have conducted ourselves in the world, and especially in our relations with you, in the holiness and sincerity that are from God. We have done so not according to worldly wisdom but according to God's grace.

Our boast is in the fact that through grace, or in this case divine enabling, we conduct ourselves in the world and with each other in the holiness and sincerity that comes from God. This is not a product of worldly wisdom or human ability but is the product of the work of grace in our lives. In other words, it doesn't happen because we have the knowledge and ability to do it on our own in the flesh. It happens as a direct result of God's work in and through us. All credit for the work goes to the only One who can enable it to happen—God. The revelation is that God's grace is the enabling factor that we need to get the job done! *God did that!*

In study we also discover that grace is our *source of supply.* This is evident in Hebrews 4:16.

> Hebrews 4:16 (NIV84)—Let us then approach the throne of grace with confidence, so that we may receive mercy and find grace to help us in our time of need.

At the throne of grace we find grace to help in time of need! It is through divine favor, influence, and power that we have the opportunity and ability to go before the throne of God and obtain everything we need for success. Throughout this verse there is an obvious emphasis on the absolute work of grace as our source of supply. Living the Grace Life is living the Blessed Life!

Long ago I set aside the idea that God wants us destitute and abandoned. Although needs vary and the idea of what constitutes a blessed life changes throughout the world and its various cultures, I maintain that God's kids are blessed kids. It doesn't matter if you are living in the suburbs of a major North American city or in a small tin roofed dwelling in the heart of a third world country, God wants you to experience the peace and comfort of his supply. Have faith in the fact that he gives resources to his children.

Even when Paul addressed the subject of giving in 2 Corinthians 9 (which we will expound on later as well), he emphasized that the resource supply in our lives is a work of grace.

> 2 Corinthians 9:6–10 (niv84)—Remember this: Whoever sows sparingly will also reap sparingly, and whoever sows generously will also reap generously. Each man should give what he has decided in his heart to give, not reluctantly or under compulsion, for God loves a cheerful giver. And God is able to make all grace abound to you, so that in all things at all times, having all that you need, you will abound in every good work. As it is written: "He has scattered abroad his gifts to the poor; his righteousness endures forever." Now he who supplies seed to the sower and bread for food will also supply and increase your store of seed and will enlarge the harvest of your righteousness.

Look closely at the concept that God supplies and increases the seed in our lives and as a result, even our giving is a work of grace! Giving of our time, talent, and treasure is as much a part of the Grace Life as anything else. Tied to the supply from grace is our willingness to cooperate with Kingdom Advance. As a part of living the Grace Life, we all need to learn the value of giving as we are led.

If you will pay close attention, the words "decided in his heart" stand out in the text. They stand out because living in grace is a matter of the heart being influenced by God. In these verses we must notice that Paul is giving the instructions that God will bless you generously if you follow his influence in your giving. Living the Grace Life in the area of giving is not just giving because you know there is a need, but giving because God's favor, influence, and power are at work in you.

What is profound to me is that you can trust what your heart is saying to you if it is surrendered to God. Matter of fact, there is no fear in giving with a surrendered heart. On the flip side, a heart that has not been surrendered to God is a dangerous thing according to Jeremiah 17:7-10.

> Jeremiah 17:7–10 (NIV84)—"But blessed is the man who trusts in the Lord, whose confidence is in him. He will be like a tree planted by the water that sends out its roots by the stream. It does not fear when heat comes; its leaves are always green. It has no worries in a year of drought and never fails to bear fruit." The heart is deceitful above all things and beyond cure. Who can understand it? "I the Lord search the heart and examine the mind, to reward a man according to his conduct, according to what his deeds deserve."

These verses show us that the heart is deceitful above all things and beyond cure. This is astounding because "all things" would even include the father of lies, Satan. This may lead you to wonder how you can trust your heart in the matter of giving if it is in fact deceitful above all things. There is a simple answer. The issue here is the matter of trusting the Lord and placing your confidence in him. This becomes a surrender issue and under grace a surrendered heart is a heart that has been mended. These verses show that a person who has surrendered their heart to God is like a fruitful tree.

If you have ever been around a fruit-bearing tree you will remember that the fruit is both the source of giving and reproducing. Of the fruit that is cast, there are seeds of reproduction in them. When we are willing to sow from the fruitful blessings in our lives, there is a promised multiplication coming back to us. It is then revealed in these verses that a person's heart is deceitful above all things. There is no doubt that this is talking about a heart that has not been surrendered to God.

Once God searches the heart and examines the mind and he finds it to be surrendered, the reward comes! A heart that has been surrendered has also been justified in the eyes of God through faith in the blood of Jesus according to Romans 3:21-26.

> Romans 3:21–26 (niv84)—But now a righteousness from God, apart from law, has been made known, to which the Law and the Prophets testify. This righteousness from God comes through faith in Jesus Christ to all who believe. There is no difference, for all have sinned and fall short of the glory of God, and are justified freely by his grace through the redemption that

came by Christ Jesus. God presented him as a sacrifice of atonement, through faith in his blood. He did this to demonstrate his justice, because in his forbearance he had left the sins committed beforehand unpunished—he did it to demonstrate his justice at the present time, so as to be just and the one who justifies those who have faith in Jesus.

That is another example of the Grace Life in action. Our justification in God's eyes is imparted to us by grace when we have faith in Jesus. The righteousness of God—not our own right actions—comes to us through faith! That mends the heart and gives it the favor, influence, and power to make the right choices. These choices include the righteous action of sowing into Kingdom purpose with our finances and other resources.

Too many people complain about having to give or even try to come up with excuses on why they don't have to give. They are not living the Grace Life and they have not surrendered their heart to God in this area. A surrendered heart knows that grace is the source of supply and that as you give God makes all grace abound to you so that in all things at all times, having all that you need, you will abound in every good work. You abound because God's grace abounds in you! Seed Faith works as the principle of sowing and reaping! We don't need to be afraid to fully surrender our hearts to God and we should always remember that a surrendered heart is a giving heart.

We are also forceful because grace is our *divine strength*. Paul understood this point well. He did not have the comfortable life of a fine home and a nice car that many preachers enjoy today in North America. His life in Christ was one of persecution and hardships. This is not to say that he didn't have good times. He said that he knew how to abound. But his story reads of one who was persecuted greatly for his faith both outside the church by those who opposed Christianity and inside the church by those who opposed his theology concerning the non-Jewish believers—notwithstanding the spiritual attacks as well. At one point we even find Paul praying for relief from one of these oppressions when a powerful word came to him in 2 Corinthians 12:9-10.

> 2 Corinthians 12:9–10 (NIV84)—But he said to me, "My grace is sufficient for you, for my power is made perfect in weakness." Therefore I will boast all the more gladly about my weaknesses, so that Christ's power may rest on me. That is why, for Christ's sake, I delight in weaknesses, in insults, in hardships, in persecutions, in difficulties. For when I am weak, then I am strong.

Wow! My heart leaps for joy as I watch Paul live the Grace Life in his New Testament writings. Paul imparted tremendous spiritual insight for all of us in this passage. Our power or strength may be weak but God's power and strength is made perfect in that environment. We find that the key to spiritual success isn't found in our strength, power, or ability, but it is found God's strength, God's power, and God's ability at work in us.

The point should be made that when you finally realize just how little you can do on your own maybe then you'll turn it over to God. We are not strong in God when we think we can stand without him. We are strong in God when we recognize total dependence on his favor, influence, and power to see us through.

We must be warned that there are a lot of Christians that "burn out" in ministry simply because they are trying to do God's work on their own ability and strength. We have all seen many talented and committed people work themselves so hard in ministry that they became unhappy and eventually quit. One reason this happens is that they lose focus on the Source and begin going through the motions of ministry on their own strength.

Pastors do that too. I have had several pastor friends run out of juice years before they should have. The daily grind of doing ministry and fulfilling ministerial obligations took its toll and they walked away from ministry for the chance to do something else. Others got so tired that they made bad decisions and felt they should leave the ministry as a result of them. The sad part is that all of this is unnecessary. We should never forget that ministry should bring joy not sorrow. It should bring life and not death. When we live and operate in the Grace Life we feel the energy and strength that comes by faith.

Keep in mind that it is easy to get exhausted in ministry when you are doing it on your own strength. Burn out happens when we burn our candle at both ends instead of relying on the fire of the Holy Spirit that resonates on the inside of our spirit. It must be true that if there was anyone that could have burned out and given up it was Paul, yet his final testimony tells the triumphal outcome in 2 Timothy 4:6-8.

> 2 Timothy 4:6–8 (NIV84)—For I am already being poured out like a drink offering, and the time has come for my departure. I have fought the good fight, I have finished the race, I have kept the faith. Now there is in store for me the crown of righteousness, which the Lord, the righteous Judge, will award to me on that day— and not only to me, but also to all who have longed for his appearing.

Paul ended his journey in a state of happiness and contentment. One thing for sure, he didn't burn out and quit. It is clear that he didn't burn out because he knew how to trust in the divine strength that was given to him in the Grace Life. When you read his story in the Book of Acts and his testimony throughout his Epistles it is clear that he worked hard, was very busy, and faced multiple persecutions. He experienced beatings, jail terms, shipwrecks, and was both received and rejected. Through all of this, he never lost heart and he never lost integrity because he knew where his strength came from.

His passion and desire for ministry burned in the fire of the Holy Spirit. He recognized that everything he had and everything he was doing was a product of the Holy Spirit and that by the Spirit he would continue forward with strength and vitality. Paul learned to completely rely on that divine strength and the result was a continuing vitality for ministry accomplishment. He did not lose strength because in the Grace Life the strength comes from God and the result was a ministry that never lost its impact. He continued until God said his assignment was through. I pray for that to be the testimony of every person reading this.

If you are involved in ministry and it has become a drudgery to continue, you need to take inventory of your present situation. Ask yourself the pointed question, "Am I doing this by grace or on my own?" If you are simply going through the motions of ministry and no longer feel it as a functioning part of your walk with God, you need to refocus! If you find yourself in an operational pattern that no longer saturates itself in prayer, you are most likely not operating in the divine strength that comes from the Grace Life.

Watch for the warning signs. One clear signal of ministry burn out is when we feel alone and have constant fantasies about quitting. People who begin to burn out tend to feel as though no one understands where they are and have strong feelings of isolation. If you ever feel this way, you need to seek spiritual advice quickly. Share these feelings with your advisor and then put into place some level of rejuvenation. This starts with a conscious decision to stop trying to do God's business under your own strength. Live the Grace Life and charge yourself with His strength and power.

By now you can see the point that I have made concerning grace taking on the various forms necessary for the Grace Life to be realized. The favor, influence, and power of the Holy Spirit are working to give to us everything we need for Kingdom productivity. The good news is that by grace we are given these things on a continual basis. Grace never has an off day! Grace never goes out of business. Grace is an eternal, always on, and always available resource generator.

Another one of those forms is grace as the *divine teacher*. This concept is found in Titus 2:11-12.

> Titus 2:11–12 (niv84)—For the grace of God that brings salvation has appeared to all men. It teaches us to say "No" to ungodliness and worldly passions, and to live self-controlled, upright and godly lives in this present age,

In this passage we find that grace teaches us to say, "No" to ungodliness and worldly passions. This goes directly with the points made in our previous two chapters. We are not saying, "No" to sin because we have a list of rules from the preacher or denomination, we are saying, "No" because divine favor, influence, and power are at work in our lives—teaching us the will and plan of God concerning those subjects!

I need to say emphatically that there is no teacher like the grace of God. Listen carefully to the next few words. It is his favor that puts us in the position, his influence that takes us in the right direction, and his power that gives us the ability to do what the Spirit is saying to do. We then become forceful because the grace of God is teaching us what to do and when to do it. On the other side of this is the fact that grace is also teaching us what not to do and when not to do it! The guidance of the Holy Spirit through grace is a tremendous dynamic of the divine teacher that grace is in our lives.

One time, I was informed of a situation in the church I pastored that needed dire attention immediately. The problem was, I was the only one that could address it but because of some of the other demands being placed on me in ministry I really didn't have the energy or desire to confront this new situation. I wanted to ignore it, although by ignoring it greater problems would arise in the very near future.

At the heart of this situation was a man whom I really liked and had never had any problems with. It would appear that a situation was arising against him and he was being influenced to do something that would be destructive if allowed to continue. I knew I needed to warn him, but I also knew my involvement would cause feelings against me to arise from the other party involved. I fought against the impression to call him and justified it by deciding I needed to talk to him in person and not over the phone. I realize now that an in person meeting with him at a later time would have been too late.

I left the house that morning having made up my mind that I would wait until I saw him at church to talk to him. I firmly purposed that I would not call him. In my heart, I had really decided to keep my hands off of this situation entirely, even though the Holy Spirit was prompting me otherwise. Leaving my neighborhood, I usually turned right in the direction toward the church. But as I pulled up to that intersection, I felt impressed to turn left and go the opposite direction of my office.

This impression was so strong that I turned left not really understanding what it meant.

At that point, I began to follow these inner urges to take certain directional turns that lead me through a large neighborhood about one mile from my house. At that time this neighborhood had a new section under construction. Winding through it, I kept wondering to myself why I was doing such a thing. Yet I felt so right in the moment that I continued on this particular path. I pulled up to a corner deep inside that neighborhood, looked to my left, and to my surprise the man I needed to talk to was standing in the middle of an empty lot.

As I pulled up, he looked at me with a surprised look and said, "What are you doing here? I really need to talk to you."

I replied, "I really need to talk to you too."

That day, on an empty lot, this man initiated the conversation that would redeem the situation. I recognized that the Holy Spirit was teaching me, even to the point of becoming my driving instructor for a few minutes. Because I was willing to follow what the Spirit was saying, I learned a valuable lesson about trusting in the Lord even when afraid of the consequences.

As the divine Teacher, he guided me to the exact place I needed to be for Kingdom purpose. I knew where to go and what to do when I got there. There is no substitute for divine favor, influence, and power when it comes to the lessons he wants to teach.

Not only does the grace of God teach us, the grace of God is also our *Divine Master Plan*. By God's favor, influence, and power we receive the blueprints necessary to build what God wants us to build out of our lives. If we will live the Grace Life, our lives will be built by God's design and not our own.

I have discovered that giving ourselves to prayer, meditating on God's word, and listening to wise counsel from Christian advisors is helpful in this process. One issue that must be settled is faith in the fact that God really does have a master plan for our lives. 1 Corinthians 3:10 shows this point powerfully.

> 1 Corinthians 3:10 (niv84)—By the grace God has given me, I laid a foundation as an expert builder, and someone else is building on it. But each one should be careful how he builds.

The example given to us by Paul was that no matter what it looked like he had done, the credit for the design and execution of the design was the work of the grace of God. God's favor allowed it to be done. God's influence directed it to be done. God's power enabled it to be done. *God did that!*

The reality stands that everything that is built in the Kingdom of God must be by God's design and not on our whims and wishes. We must never lose sight of the fact that God's plan is a really great plan and when it is by God's design there is peace in the final outcome. God's plan is the best plan because he is the Master Architect. We know this and yet many times we don't allow him to be what he is—the one with the master plan. It is very interesting to notice in the scriptures how easy it is for people to leave his plan and take matters into their own hands. Clearly, Israel of the

Old Testament didn't always follow God's design, but he did give them the promise of its reality in Jeremiah 29:11.

> Jeremiah 29:11 (NIV84)—For I know the plans I have for you," declares the Lord, "plans to prosper you and not to harm you, plans to give you hope and a future.

Looking at God's dealings with the Children of Israel, it is easy to discern that God's master plan was always available to them even when they lapsed into doing things their own way for years. God let them know that he had a plan for them, and it was an awesome plan! That really is a picture of New Testament grace in the Old Testament. The good news for us is that we can claim that same promise in our lives today through grace. God's plan for us is to prosper us and not to harm us. He has a plan to give us hope and a future and it's a bright future at that.

I can remember when we were going through the transitional change from the Pentecostal denomination I had more questions than answers. It seemed that everything in our lives had been turned upside down, and we were left to rebuild without even knowing what it should look like. People who had been influential in our former congregation were leaving, and everything in the church was beginning to take a different shape. It was during this time that I found myself praying in the church auditorium and asking God what this "new" congregation was going to look like. I wanted to know them when I saw them.

This was especially important to me in light of having been in a denomination where everyone and everything has a distinctive, "cookie-cutter" look and emphasis. I was really trying to figure out what the culture of our new church would be. At that moment the Holy Spirit impressed on my heart to stand in the pulpit and to look across the empty seats that were now before me. In a flash, I felt these words in my spirit, "I want you to preach to blessed people and to pastor happy people." It was that simple.

Blessed and happy has been an underlying slogan for our church since then and we see it flesh out every week in our congregation. That doesn't mean that we don't have people that go through times of trials and sadness. What it means to us is that we are striving to create a church culture that encourages hope, healing, peace, and joy even in difficult times. This also helps us maintain a church environment where people are accepted where they are and are allowed to grow in Christ at their own pace.

That pointed focus—blessed and happy—has helped me to preach and teach specifically to the church according to God's direction for us as a community of believers. It gave us a blueprint to follow. Blessed and happy is a culture mentality and for us it is a huge part of living the Grace Life. Using this as a master plan directive we have tailored our teaching, preaching, and ministry vision in such a way as to produce this as the end result. To some this may seem too simplistic, but to us it is the essence of a divine master plan for our church that was given to us by grace.

Revealed in Jeremiah 29:11 is also the beautiful promise that no matter what the circumstances look like, God still has a plan and it is a good one. This is especially important to remember during those times when we don't understand what is happening in our lives. Just remembering that God's plan is still in action will help us keep the faith during difficult moments and uncertain times. If God hasn't quit, neither should we. This again is the kind of perseverance that comes through living the Grace Life.

I have discovered this first hand on several occasions but one instance stands out in particular. Raylene and I had a difficult year in 2007. It seemed that the pain of transition was finally coming to an end while a bitter attack against us was launched. Everything from personal assaults by people to the scare of cancer in our family seemed to come in waves that year. In the midst of it all, I had a powerful word given to me concerning the vision of the church and was working diligently on a focused direction for our ministry initiatives.

As the year was drawing to a close, I had everything in order to launch the new vision in January of 2008. I felt very excited that we would finally have a purpose statement and a ministry vision directive that articulated the way I felt God wanted us to operate as a church. The new flow chart had at its top the designated titles of those who were considered pastoral leadership with their names and ministry oversight underneath. The first names of course were Raylene's and mine under the title of Lead Pastors. Following this were the various names and titles for Teaching Pastor, Youth Pastor,

Music Pastor, Children Pastor, and Administrative Assistant. At the end of the line was a couple that had nothing but a question mark above and below their name. I knew they would be on our Pastoral team, I just didn't know at that moment what their title would be or what they would be pastorally overseeing.

As we ended the month of November, I was ramping everything up for the launch in January of the new vision. I felt in my heart that we would finally be able to launch in the new direction that we had been working towards for years. This was our moment! I was not prepared for, nor did I have any expectancy for, what happened next. December 2, 2007 is engraved in the halls of my memory. In one moment on that day, every name between our names and the question mark couple had to have an eraser taken to them.

Three couples, all who were to fill the key roles in the ministry flowchart, told me of their intention to leave the church at the beginning of the next year for other ministry opportunities. I was shocked to say the least. These couples had been with us for years. They had been our friends for a long time! With the exception of the teaching pastor, I had no idea they would even consider leaving. Even in the teaching pastor's case, I expected he would remain until we had the new vision firmly established. As it stood, he felt that since the others were leaving now, it would be best for it to all happen at once, sparing the church another departure a few months later. *BAM!* Just like that, nothing but my wife, a question mark couple, and me on the flowchart of pastoral ministry at our church. We had no teaching pastor, youth pastor, children pastor, administrative assistant, or worship pastor.

My immediate response that day was one of distraught disappointment. I was more than hurt; I fell into a state of hopelessness almost instantaneously. These couples not only represented our pastoral leadership, they were our platform staff as well. I was left to launch a new vision in four weeks without a drummer, keyboardist, bassist, and guitarist as well as none of the pastoral roles mentioned before. One month from launching our vision, the board was erased—leaving a question mark and us. As you might be able to imagine, I had a huge question mark in my head! I said to them verbally as we met for more than three hours after church that day that I might as well leave too.

In my mind, it was over. How could I launch the new vision now? How would we even operate as a church without all of these vital roles being filled? I paced the auditorium wondering why another church in town deserved my team! I kept asking what I had done wrong to deserve this. We left that day to part ways in ministry. They left to a vision of hope and excitement, as another church in our community would expand ministry through them. I left in hopeless despair believing that we would not and could not survive this one. That is the way I saw it while being closed minded to the Grace Life that was trying to happen around me.

As it so happened, the question mark couple had taken our two boys home with them that day. We arrived at their house to pick the boys up in an obvious state of dejection. Immediately, they inquired as to what had happened and we began to fill them in on the day's revelation. Bryan and Misty stepped away from the question mark position that day. What happened next became the catalyst for the miraculous. After going through my doubt and despair while sitting on their couch, Misty leaned forward and asked me a pointed question. "Do you really think God is surprised by this?" It struck me right where it needed to!

This couple then declared that God did this! While I was talking about waiting to present the vision, they countered with the idea that if God said for me to launch it in January, and he knew this was going to happen, then why would I move off of the plan. They spoke faith to us that God had all of the people we needed in place, we just needed to find them. And find them we did! Grace gave us the master plan before the week was out.

Every one of the couples that left our staff that year have gone on to find the blessing of the Lord in their lives. One thing that I am deeply grateful for is that we did not part in anger or with malice. Although I was hurt, I released them with my blessing and I am glad to say that we have remained friends. Ironically enough, even today before writing these words I played golf with one of them. They are blessed and so are we. Looking back I realize God had a plan for them and a plan for us. That is the beauty of the Grace Life.

In case you are wondering, we did launch the new vision in January 2008. We also had a new band, a new worship style that went well with the vision, and a new ministry structure with fresh minds. Since then, every aspect of the ministry team on that flowchart has expanded. Both our pastoral team and our platform staff fit the vision, and we have a better situation now than we had before. Those couples needed to be released to follow God's plan for their lives, and we needed them to be released in order to follow his plan in the life of our church. Instead of being discouraged, I should have been excited. God was releasing us to our destiny according to his master plan—and his plan was and is a good plan. He has prospered us in a marvelous way, and knowing what we know now, I wouldn't want it any other way!

Keep in mind that faith plays an important role when it comes to the plan revealed by grace. Many times it will seem impossible. There will also be times of discouragement and confusion. What I learned through this experience is that God's plan is always good even if the water is rough on the way there. The Grace Life way is the way of perseverance! We have God's favor, influence, and power working overtime to see us through to the ultimate destination God has planned for us.

I know I've focused primarily on the work of grace in our spiritual lives directed in ministry and Kingdom activities, but this principle is true even in the areas our personal lives that are not directly related to Kingdom activity. Too many times we set out to build with our own design in mind thinking we know exactly what we want and exactly how to get it. We go after positions and jobs without really seeking spiritual guidance. We make life altering decisions from a natural perspective rather than seeking the mind of God.

What we will find is that this often leads to frustration and to something less than God had planned for us. Psalm 127:1 gives insight into the fact that if the Lord doesn't build the house the builders are laboring in vain. The fact of the matter is that if God doesn't build it, it isn't really getting done in the most expedient way. It is when we take over the building process that we labor in vain! We may get a result, but it is not the result God had in mind. True success dictates that there must be a work of the Spirit in everything that we do. Our building must be done according to God's master plan given to us by grace.

Some may wonder how to know this master plan given by the Spirit. I have discovered that among other things, I can tap into God's master plan through prayer, meditation on God's word, and seeking godly counsel with people that I can trust. When we surrender to the Grace Life there is a calm assurance that comes with following God's directives. We are forceful when we build under divine favor, influence, and power. What we must realize is that our ability to operate in the Kingdom of God is totally dependant on the work of grace in our lives. When we rely on grace, rather than our own ability and strength, we become forceful people operating in a forcefully advancing Kingdom—the Kingdom of God! *God did that so that I can do this!*

Chapter Five

GRACE MAKES US FRUITFUL

"Are Dave and Karen enough?" Those were the words I heard sitting in the side bleacher seat in a packed out Christian concert with several thousand people in attendance. The Holy Spirit was moving heavy on my heart that night. My family had been invited to this concert by a couple from our church that had become as much family to us as anyone blood related. Dave and Karen even gained the lofty status of G'ma and G'pa to our boys and had been with us at Triumph for several years at this point. They came to our church after having been un-churched for some twenty years. I had the privilege, as their pastor, to watch them grow in their faith and love for the Lord. Now sitting with them in this concert, God was dealing with me. And he needed to. You might be thinking, "What does this have to do with the Grace Life?" Hold on for a moment and we will get there!

This concert experience had me somewhat frustrated. To be honest, I get that way sometimes. I have dreams of pastoring a growing church. A vibrant church! I dream of a packed house with relevant ministry! My idea of success might be tied just a little to how many people are showing up on a regular basis and calling our church their home—which can be misguided. Going to this concert and seeing all of these people gathered for worship reminded me of just how small we were as a local congregation.

That night I was overwhelmed with the feeling of insignificance. I was sitting there, with tears running down my face in God's presence, asking myself if the years and the tears really amounted to anything worthwhile. We had gone through a lot of pain to found Triumph as a non-denominational church. As noted before, we lost some dear friends and had family turn their back on us in the process. All of this is the making of a pity party if you know what I mean. That is, a pity party for those who don't understand the Grace Life.

Here at this concert, God was teaching me! Sitting in my feelings of insignificance God asked me again, "Are Dave and Karen enough?" Looking at them worshipping down the row of seats from me, I could see their transformed lives. Evident was the miraculous work of God upon them. I remembered suddenly the healing that Karen had received from a childhood laced with fear, abandonment, and abuse and the joy of a renewed zeal for the Kingdom of God that rested on Dave's glowing countenance. At that moment, the implication of the question was clear.

If all we had to show for the labor and pain that surrounded the establishing of our church was the transformation in this one couple, was it worth the price? What if there was never a big crowd? What if the ministry God had given me was to remain in obscurity for its entire duration? At the end of the day, was the mighty work done in this one couple worth the price we had paid? "Are Dave and Karen enough?" My heart sprang into action as my answer came forth. "Yes Lord, Dave and Karen are enough! I don't need a crowd, I am satisfied with them." If the church I pastored was going to grow beyond its present state, I had to come to a place of accepting that.

That is what living the Grace Life can do for you. Grace makes us free, grace makes us forceful, and grace also makes us fruitful. The lesson that I needed to learn is that we are not responsible for the parameters of the fruit, God is! The harvest is totally up to him. I was frustrated because I didn't understand this principle. The fact is that living the Grace Life produces fruit, but I must be comfortable in knowing that the good works that I have done through grace gives God the opportunity to bring increase as he sees fit.

I realize now that it is very easy to focus on a harvest that is not meant for you right now. I was feeling sorry about the lack of a crowd causing me to forget the miracle of Dave and Karen that was created in the church environment produced through the pain of birth and transition. I had to reconcile the fact that if Dave and Karen where the only fruit of this endeavor, it was still worth it! This is addressed perfectly in 1 Corinthians 3:5-10.

> 1 Corinthians 3:5–10 (NIV84)—What, after all, is Apollos? And what is Paul? Only servants, through whom you came to believe—as the Lord has assigned to each his task. I planted the seed, Apollos watered it, but God made

it grow. So neither he who plants nor he who waters is anything, but only God, who makes things grow. The man who plants and the man who waters have one purpose, and each will be rewarded according to his own labor. For we are God's fellow workers; you are God's field, God's building. By the grace God has given me, I laid a foundation as an expert builder, and someone else is building on it. But each one should be careful how he builds.

Here we find grace influencing one to plant and another to water but the growth—or increase—is from God. Our responsibility is to act upon the grace influence in our lives and do what the Spirit is leading us to do. The responsibility of fruit is God's part! Grace says, "Build it." God determines its size. Grace says, "Plant it." God determines how much is harvested.

The point I am trying to stress is that when we get too focused on the parameters of the harvest we lose sight of the call to follow the Holy Spirit and do the things He is telling us to do. I have seen many people stop following the influence of grace all together because they became dissatisfied with the timing and quantity of the fruit. Many times their dissatisfaction was the product of looking at the fruit in someone else's life and allowing jealousy and envy to rise in their hearts. An understanding of the Grace Life will guard our hearts from this debilitating mindset.

I have come to understand that the Grace Life is living in the joy of knowing that God brings the fruit when we act on grace, and we can trust that our hearts will be satisfied in him. 2 Corinthians 8:6-7 gives us this insight in regards to our actions.

> 2 Corinthians 8:6–7 (NIV84)—So we urged Titus, since he had earlier made a beginning, to bring also to completion this act of grace on your part. But just as you excel in everything— in faith, in speech, in knowledge, in complete earnestness and in your love for us—see that you also excel in this grace of giving.

Paul calls the good works an act of grace and it is clear that these actions are producing fruit. Put in another way, acts of grace on our part produce Kingdom fruit on God's part! In this passage we find that even our giving is an act of grace. Divine favor, influence, and power are causing us to give. I can fully appreciate the words used by Paul, "This grace of giving."

What we must realize is that those who act on grace find themselves rich in all ways in Christ. The Grace Life causes us to become rich monetarily (having all that we need), rich in ministry (seeing people healed and souls won), rich in joy (having the joy of the Lord), rich in peace (peace from God not circumstances), and rich in satisfaction (our fulfillment is in him). The Grace life makes you fruitful to the point that you excel in everything! When you speak, you do it as one who speaks God's words. When you serve, you do it with the strength God gives. When you give, it's by God's resources and God's ability working in you. By this, God gets all the credit for the fruit!

If we are going to be instrumental in Kingdom Advance we must raise the level of our faith to believe that God wants us to be fruitful in his purpose. This mentality also releases us from the temptation of greedy gain. When we realize that the blessings are for a higher purpose we have a conduit mentality rather than a hoarding mentality. Blessings are meant to flow through us for the greater good of Kingdom Advance and not hoarded by us for selfish ambition. Keep in mind that God intends on us being fruitful and he has given us everything we need to accomplish his purpose on Earth. Jesus made this point clear in John 15:16.

> John 15:16 (NIV84)—You did not choose me, but I chose you and appointed you to go and bear fruit—fruit that will last. Then the Father will give you whatever you ask in my name.

Every person in the church has been chosen and appointed to go and bear fruit. It is a part of our Christian DNA. No one who is truly part of God's church can say that they have become part of the church but are not responsible to bear fruit. That doesn't even make sense! God did not call us, save us, and empower us for fruitlessness. The Kingdom of God advances through people who understand we have been called, chosen, and sent as bearers of lasting fruit.

Those people who get this concept deep in their spirit will accomplish God's purpose on the Earth. We are supposed to bear Kingdom fruit in our lives by the grace of God as a part of the high calling of Christ. Kingdom fruit comes when we act on divine favor, divine influence, and divine power and when we accomplish the things that he has called us to do. We must always remember that we have been called to do good things. When we sow a little, we reap in proportion a little. When we sow much, we reap in proportion much! Either way, God is still in charge of the harvest.

One thing to keep in mind is that the secret to successful fruit bearing is to recognize it is the fruit born by Grace Works and not by our own works. If we do not recognize this foundational truth, we try to bear fruit on our own, and that never works. I have found over the years that are many instances where people are less than fruitful for Kingdom purpose because they try to bear Kingdom fruit on their own ability, desire, and strength. It is evident that this type of self-work activity only leads to frustration and hopelessness.

We need to admit once and for all that we do not have what it takes to bear Kingdom fruit on our own. I want to affirm that this declaration is not meant to be a negative declaration. This is a positive reinforcement of fruitful living in the Grace Life. To denounce our own ability to perform without God must precede our declaration of surrender to his grace activity in and through us. Kingdom Advance is here and with it comes Kingdom fruit! Let grace make you fruitful for Kingdom purpose! The Kingdom of God is forcefully advancing, and we are forceful people who are also fruitful people. In the end, we need to realize it is God-fruit that counts! And yes, Dave and Karen are enough! *God did that so that I can do this!*

Chapter Six

GREAT GRACE

The early church had a dynamic working for them concerning grace that has been lost in many modern day church environments. It is hard to imagine what it must have been like—an organic culture of believers that grew rapidly yet met the individual needs of each one in their Christian community. In that environment, great miracles were taking place and unity abounded everywhere. When reading about the early church, one could say that the unity they experienced would be amazing all by itself—notwithstanding the miracles and selfless sacrifice. These people were absolutely together in unison, which in my estimation is miraculous. Acts 4:31-35 gives a picture of their reality.

> Acts 4:31–35 (NIV84)—After they prayed, the place where they were meeting was shaken. And they were all filled with the Holy Spirit and spoke the word of God boldly. All the believers were one in heart and mind. No one claimed that any of his possessions was his own, but they shared everything they had. With great power the apostles continued to testify to the resurrection of the Lord Jesus, and much grace was upon them all. There were no needy

persons among them. For from time to time those who owned lands or houses sold them, brought the money from the sales and put it at the apostles' feet, and it was distributed to anyone as he had need.

As you can see, this is an awesome picture. They were filled with the Holy Spirit, they spoke the word of God boldly, and they shared everything they had! What we see here is a beautiful display of unity and harmony in the church that was truly of one heart and one mind. Of note is the fact that there was sufficient provision for everyone, great power was working among them, and the people were not afraid to participate in sacrificial giving.

Pay close attention to the fact that all of this came as the result of "much grace" being upon all of them. Much grace! Not just a small amount of grace but much. Some translations even go as far as to translate this as, "Great grace." The strong implication is that they were fully committed to a Grace Life experience. If there is anything we need today, that is it! There is plenty of evidence to show that the only way the early church accomplished what they did was through much divine favor, influence, and power working in them, resulting in their willingness to surrender to God's plan.

Much grace also created among them two vital areas for effective ministry. They operated with *a community of love* and *a culture of generosity*. If effective ministry is a priority, we must never forget that the Kingdom of God operates on a team mentality saturated with these two elements. Matter of fact, both of these vital areas are only cultivated through a team dynamic. What we do together for Kingdom Advance far exceeds what any one of us could do by ourselves.

By paying close attention to this dynamic in the early church, you will see that the picture we get is that of an organic body working in tandem and not of single member entities working separately and alone. Paul and Peter, who had powerful ministry anointing, demonstrated this team necessity by surrounding themselves with other Christians in ministry campaigns. They built bridges between cultures and brought people together for Kingdom Advance. They understood the power of togetherness.

It can also be demonstrated that the operation of the early church proves that grace is intensified through team. As the team expanded, so did the effects of grace until it could only be described as "much" or "great" grace resting upon them. There is a lesson to be learned here. If we are going to intensify our Kingdom productivity we must realize that operating under grace pulls us together in love whereas operating on human effort alone often produces factions and solitary campaigns. If there are factions in the church you can rest assured that more flesh and less grace is in control of the community.

The first area to cover is that grace produces *a community of love*. Such is the very identifier of discipleship according to John 13:34-35.

> John 13:34–35 (NIV84)— "A new command I give you: Love one another. As I have loved

you, so you must love one another. By this all men will know that you are my disciples, if you love one another."

Ponder the idea that we will be identified as disciples because we love one another. In these verses we see that the essence of true Christian unity is that there is no room for anything less than authentic love one for another. It would be easy to think that miracles, signs, wonders, or the preaching of the gospel would be the strongest indicators of discipleship—especially since these things are emphasized so strongly in many church environments. But in reality, all of these things hold little value if the church is overrun with hate, jealousy, envy, strife, bitterness, and factions. Paul addressed this very concept in 1 Corinthians 13:1-8.

> 1 Corinthians 13:1–8 (NIV84)—If I speak in the tongues of men and of angels, but have not love, I am only a resounding gong or a clanging cymbal. If I have the gift of prophecy and can fathom all mysteries and all knowledge, and if I have a faith that can move mountains, but have not love, I am nothing. If I give all I possess to the poor and surrender my body to the flames, but have not love, I gain nothing. Love is patient, love is kind. It does not envy, it does not boast, it is not proud. It is not rude, it is not self-seeking, it is not easily angered, it keeps no record of wrongs. Love does not delight in evil but rejoices with the truth. It always protects, always trusts, always hopes, always perseveres. Love never fails. But where there are prophecies,

they will cease; where there are tongues, they
will be stilled; where there is knowledge, it will
pass away.

He is clearly teaching that if the church has not
developed a community of love, it doesn't really matter
how high the level of spiritual gifts and Christian service
is among them as believers. He emphatically declares
that you can speak in tongues and prophesy, you can
give every thing to the poor and do the miraculous by
faith, but if you are not a community of love it is all
for nothing.

Those are strong words yet they hold high value
even today. I believe that today's church needs to
develop, by grace, a community of love that is patient,
kind, and without envy, boasting, and selfish pride! Our
church environments should be without anger, jealousy,
or selfish ambition. What about having a church
that doesn't hold grudges and is not saturated with
untruthful gossip? I want to be a part of a church like
that! A church that protects and builds a community
of trust, hope, and perseverance is a Grace Life church.

Building a church community with this kind of love
produces the other vital area for effective ministry—*a
culture of generosity*. When we truly love, we become
generous. This is true in every facet of life including the
church. When love takes center stage in our hearts, we
become generous with our resources and we will go to
great lengths to provide for those to whom this love is
directed. We will literally give the shirt off our backs
to them.

Think about the generosity produced in love that gives the last portion of food to a loved one. I have done that with my children. There have been times that I wasn't full but freely gave what I had left to them so that they would be. How about those who have been so generous in love that they gave their lives protecting their loved ones? We have all heard of instances were a loving parent was willing to give his or her life to protect their child. As we see, loving parents build a culture of generosity towards their children because they dwell in a community of love.

Although this is not a book about marriage relationships let me throw this out for consideration, healthy marital relationships are rooted in both love and generosity. If a marriage is not built on a community of love and a culture of generosity towards each other then the door is open for malice, bitterness, and separation. Think about that as we discover that the same is true in the church!

When there is no love and generosity in the church all you have left is push and shove, position and politics, and a general "What's in it for me?" spirit of selfishness. This needs to come alive in our spirit! If we are going to truly be effective for Kingdom Advance we must allow a culture of generosity to take hold through a community of love and we must push back against anything that is less than that. This was perfectly exampled in the description of the church given in Acts 2:41-47.

> Acts 2:41–47 (niv84)—Those who accepted his message were baptized, and about three thousand were added to their number that

day. They devoted themselves to the apostles' teaching and to the fellowship, to the breaking of bread and to prayer. Everyone was filled with awe, and many wonders and miraculous signs were done by the apostles. All the believers were together and had everything in common. Selling their possessions and goods, they gave to anyone as he had need. Every day they continued to meet together in the temple courts. They broke bread in their homes and ate together with glad and sincere hearts, praising God and enjoying the favor of all the people. And the Lord added to their number daily those who were being saved.

You can't help but see that they were a community of love with a culture of generosity. They set aside their differences for the greater cause of the Kingdom. They also climbed off of the social and economic ladders to level the playing field for everyone. There were no big "I's" and little "You's." Their generosity even went to the level of selling their possessions and distributing the money equally as needed.

Before you misunderstand the intention stated here for our purpose, I understand that the cultural and social parameters were different for the early church than for many of us today. Becoming a Christian in their paradigm often meant losing everything including family relationships, inheritances, jobs, and homes. The early church solved this problem through a community of love and a culture of generosity.

Although the particular actions of communal distribution of property and money may not be necessary in every church environment today, the willing attitude to follow the Spirit's leading in this manner is necessary. They were willing to completely surrender to the Grace Life! The church of today needs this kind of team mentality as well. The good news is that living the Grace Life does just that! It brings love and generosity to the forefront of our lives for the purpose of Kingdom Advance and the greater good of everyone.

Not only did they see this, the effect of great grace on the people also brought miracles, miraculous provision, and true fellowship! They had no problem eating together, praying together, praising together, and walking the Christian journey together. Only later, when people allowed schisms, prejudice, and fear to take precedence over grace, do we see trouble stir among the church. You can rest assured that when there is a community of love and a culture of generosity in the church, grace is being allowed to work.

For emphasis let me state again that the early church saw what they saw, they had what they had, and they accomplished what they accomplished as a direct result of great grace. They had much divine favor, influence, and power working in and through them. It is also true that they could have done many of the same things begrudgingly and under their own ability under law—where they manufactured works by themselves. If this had been the case, I am convinced that they would not have seen the dynamic fruit of God's blessing in the same magnitude.

On the other hand, seeing that these "good works" were done under much grace, they saw much fruit and experienced great blessing! When people operate under much divine favor, influence, and power many things happen that would have otherwise been stopped by fleshly pursuits and selfish ambition. It is awesome to witness that spiritual fruit has a way of growing among people who live the Grace Life. This doesn't just affect the corporate church. Those who abound in grace witness spiritual fruit and the blessing of God on a corporate level and on a personal level.

Back in the early 1990s I had the opportunity to preach in a small community church in New Brunswick, Canada. There had been some level of disunity in this church for some time as the people were divided in cliques mostly along lines of long held grudges and various negative family dynamics. The people in that church were pitted against each other in either cross family rivalries or cross family feuds. On top of this, the church had a bad political structure. Church politics was so rampant that the bylaws demanded that the people hold an election for pastor every year.

As this series of services began, the pastor confessed to me that he was coming up for election again and felt it would go against him because of the particular voting roster tilt at the present time. He simply had the wrong people against him (or the wrong people for him) at the wrong time. If you can imagine, the voting block for him could change at any moment with a simple statement in a sermon or as the result of accepting an invitation for dinner on a particular week. I had never heard of such a thing and was quite taken back by the prospects of dishonor given to the office of pastor in that church. He was literally at the mercy of the feuds while feeling in his heart that his job there as pastor was not through.

Needless to say, something needed to break among them! It was amazing to watch these people as they stood in opposition to each other—even in worship. The church and the people were divided into two sections of pews with a center aisle in the middle. Inevitably, if one side clapped with vigor the other side would be less enthusiastic in an obvious way. The final night of the series of services arrived with no change in the current situation. I will never forget that something happened that night that changed everything.

As I began to preach, you could feel a shift in the environment! There was a stirring in the hearts of some of the influencers in that audience. Divine favor, influence, and power were invading the building and a different Spirit was taking over. When I felt this shift, I began to encourage the people to move out and do what the Holy Spirit was telling them to do. At that point, a lady got up from the right side and stepped over to the left side where she grabbed another lady by the arm and said something to the effect that it was time to apologize.

This had been the very rift that had influenced that church's division for years! The other lady looked stunned and then stood up. I really didn't know what to expect at that point but to my relief they began to hug and pray for each other. I will never forget as one of them exclaimed, "I love you!" I can only describe what happened next as holy pandemonium!

The place lit up with the fire of the Holy Spirit and the release of raw human emotion. In the end, there was a powerful demonstration of the Holy Spirit as people were filled, healed, and delivered. A dozen people were baptized that night! There were more than two-dozen salvations. At the end of the service some two hours after the center aisle restoration, I was sitting on the edge of the platform, and one of the their long standing board members told me that if this is what it felt like to be saved he had never been saved before that night!

To top off the events, the pastor was no longer in jeopardy of being fired nor was he in bondage to the political pressure in the church. For the first time in years, many of these people experienced the Grace Life even if we didn't understand the concept. The immediate impact of this was nothing short of a miracle. Not only were people saved, the whole demeanor of the people that were involved in that church changed for the better. It was clear that a great weight had been lifted off of them! They became instantly happy.

I will never forget the changed countenances on the faces of the people after church. They were not only blessed spiritually, their physical lives were blessed as well as they went home free of bitterness and strife. I have often wondered what these people missed out on through the years as a result of their disunity and malice towards each other. They could have had this new level of happiness all along if they had just made better choices concerning their attitudes and actions.

I am thankful that the Grace Life was unleashed on them that night. God can do great things when great grace in upon the people. It is truly liberating.

The influence of grace produced a different result than they had been experiencing. The reality of life is that what we allow to influence us generally dictates our attitudes and actions. The fact of the matter is that we are all under the influence of something or someone to varying degrees. In our world, there are so many sources of influence we often don't even notice them. From commercials on television to the effects of friendships and mentors, influencers are all around us vying for our attention. I am not trying to say that all of the other influences are bad, I am simply pointing out that we must be very careful, and very aware, of how much influence we allow these things to have over us.

It should be of no surprise that people have influence. Problems have influence as well. What is the driving influence generally steers the direction in which we go. As far as the church goes, it is in environments of overbearing human influence that the work of God lags or even ceases. This is why we need to seek great grace and in turn strive to limit the human influence that creates a heavier reliance on human strength and ability. Living the Grace Life in its fullest is to allow for great grace to come upon you in such a way as to follow his plan and witness great results. You will find that one of the secrets to spiritual success is to rely on the Holy Spirit and his influence in the process of doing his will. This chases away the idea that you must work harder on your own in order to merit God's blessing. It also removes the spirit of fear that what is being asked of you is too much for you to handle. When grace is the driving force confidence abounds in our hearts and we know the work will get done.

As God's grace unfolds in our lives we begin to experience more! I am not saying that the favor of God can be expanded. The favor of God is settled in Christ therefore the favor of God is the favor of God! So when we speak of great grace we are not saying that there is more favor for some and less for others. The favor of God is firmly set in the sacrifice that his Son, Jesus Christ, did for all. Our actions or attitudes cannot change that.

But the same is not true about the influence and power of the Holy Spirit. In truth, these two aspects of grace can be affected by our actions and attitudes. What I am saying is that we have the capability to limit the influence and power of the Holy Spirit in our lives. If we are going to live in the success of the Grace Life, we must be willing to follow and submit to the influence of the Holy Spirit and we must also be willing to yield our will to his power. I have found that someone can stand firmly in divine favor as a child of God but then operate below the full blessing of his influence and power— simply by refusing to submit to the continuing work of grace in his or her life.

If we don't follow through, then it doesn't matter how much God is influencing and empowering us to do. It is also true that it really doesn't matter how much favor we have if we never respond to it. The point I am stressing is that the favor, influence, and power of God are all accessed by faith and are released through willful surrender. The more we surrender, the more we see his influence and power work in our lives. This willful surrender is joyous in the fact that once we surrender to Him we are no longer on our own.

This was one of the most incredible revelations that came to me as I was being released from a life of legalistic theology. The Grace Life releases us—in divine favor—from having to do the will of God in our own! The more we rest in his favor and submit to his influence and power, the more we will see the blessings of grace flow in our lives. As we submit, more and more, we see more! Just like the early church, much grace—*great grace*—can be upon us and with great grace comes great results! Much fruit! Much power! Much resource! Much healing! Much blessing!

I am fully persuaded that this is a picture of the church that Jesus came to build. I also believe that this is the kind of Christian we are supposed to be. As we live in much grace and as we see great results, Kingdom Advance is propagated in the world in a great way. Just as a moving boat leaves a wake—the evidence that it moved though that place—everywhere we go there is supposed to be a "wake"—evidence that we moved through there as the people of God! This is the essence of Mark 16:17 in the NKJV.

> Mark 16:17 (NKJV)—And these signs will follow those who believe: In My name they will cast out demons; they will speak with new tongues;

The signs should accompany and follow every believer. God's intent for each of us is that we become carriers of divine demonstration. Just as people become carriers of certain diseases and ultimately infect the world around them, we should strive to infect our world with the gospel of Jesus Christ and the demonstration of the wonder working power of our living God. The healthy New Testament church is filled with people who understand the Grace Life is a life of divine demonstration flowing through the believer into the world that surrounds them. The Apostles had miracles, love, and generosity following them! What is following you? Let's make a goal that we see divine demonstration following us. Leave a wake! Let the world know that a Kingdom Advancer has been there. The Grace Life gives us the favor, influence, and power of God to make a difference everywhere we go. Come on great grace! *God did that so that I can do this!*

Chapter Seven

GOD DID THAT

God did that! This is a thought that we need to remember, and hopefully I have planted it deep in your spirit. In living the Grace Life, this idea becomes the focal point of existence. When we understand that God did that, it means that we did not do that—at least not on our own. Although the action flowed through us, all of the necessary resources for that action come from God. It was his favor, influence, and power that made it possible. It's a grace thing!

This is a pivotal understanding for the Grace Life, especially when there is so much animosity in Christian circles concerning the idea of works in the Christian life. I need to state clearly that if we are going to accomplish Kingdom Advance, we must answer the tension that has been created by incorrect theologies that tend to pit grace against the fruitful works that accompany it. Grace is not the enemy of the fruitful works that are exampled in life action.

As a point of reference, the term I use to describe the fruitful works that accompany grace is, "Grace Works." Grace Works are those things that we do as a result of the work of grace in our lives. They are the by-product of God's favor, influence, and power and are not what we do on the front end to earn it. The important difference between self works under law and Grace Works is that we don't do these things because we are so great and know how to get things done, we do them because God has influenced us and given us the power to do the task!

We are not good on our own merit and we cannot accomplish God's business by our own ability. The truth is that if there is any good thing in us, it is the goodness of God! What is lost many times in translation is that grace does not cancel out the fact that there is a responsibility for us to act upon God's influence and power, which produces Grace Works!

Spiritual fruit comes from the Grace Works that are accomplished through our lives. This understanding is that grace produces righteous action on our part, we are doing the things that the Holy Spirit is influencing us to do and is giving us the power to do. If this is going to happen, one of the first things that we must establish is to fully understand that God is the source for everything good in our lives.

I admit that I sometimes struggle with this tension of supply and demand. My life demands and I begin to look for the supply in the natural realm. Many times my natural eyes look to physical resources—finances, possessions, people, and programs—that are available around me before I even consider taking it to the Lord in prayer. I then begin to deduct how these things can be used to take care of the present demands that I am facing.

Those things are easy to find yet they can also hide the true Source from our view. It is easy to fall into the trap of thinking that our job, or our bank account, or our contacts, are the source for the answer to our present needs. Because the physical things around us are so tangible to our senses, it is common to begin to believe that these resources are actually the source. We trust them even though they have disappointed us on many occasions. That is the point! In reality, these resources are the product given to us by the Source and cannot be relied upon as though they were the Source. This is where the tension begins.

The resources around us are the blessings of God—who is the Source of it all! In living the Grace Life, there is a mental and spiritual shift to the kind of faith that recognizes the blessings of God that surround us as just that, the blessings of God. In the Grace Life we don't rely on the blessings nor do we worship them. Our focus is on the God of the blessings!

As we grow in the Grace Life we also become more aware of the surrounding blessings of God. These blessings are no longer lost in the crowd of obligations and opportunities. We no longer pass them by as we focus on trouble and need or even on provision and prosperity. When we live the Grace Life, we see what God is doing and giving all around us. Everywhere we look we see God at work. These things are not the product of something or someone else; they are the product of God's mercy and presence in our lives. At this point, God becomes evident in the details. The focal passage of this idea is James 1:17.

> James 1:17 (NIV84)—Every good and perfect gift is from above, coming down from the Father of the heavenly lights, who does not change like shifting shadows.

This verse states that we have a consistent God who is the absolute source of everything good and perfect. It stands to reason that if everything good and perfect comes from him, then every good and perfect resource that we have is included in that list. God is the source of all resources. Our faith explodes when we realize, "God did that." People didn't do that. Bank accounts didn't do that. Occupations didn't do that. Having the right contacts didn't do that. Talent and abilities didn't do that. God did that!

This mentality has become a driving force in my life during discouraging times. As I have stated before and will also address later, we went through some difficulty while transitioning away from the denomination-centered ministry. During one of the most trying times, I began to question whether or not I was truly in God's will when accepting that original church. I kept asking myself whether or not this was truly God's plan or did I miss him.

I had been confident before, but now my confidence was waning in the face of criticism, attacks, and decreasing membership in the church. On more than one occasion I wondered if we would even make it, as family and friends turned their backs on us and walked away. I was also having some internal strife on our core pastoral team that was completely unrelated to the other difficulties we were facing. It was truly one of those, "When it rains, it pours" moments.

I look back and realize that we really needed the concept of the Grace Life, but we had very little understanding of this at that time. I was hurting and was under constant stress. It seemed that everything that I was so sure of before was in a fog of discouragement that led to doubt and fear. I lost focus and was judging the circumstance and myself by what I was doing and the results it was bringing. Keep in mind as well that this was the programming I had operated under for more than thirty years. To make matters worse, many of the people that I believed in were separating their fellowship and companionship from me. Under the old paradigm this proved in their eyes that I was wrong and God had forsaken me. I felt alone and destitute for sure.

It was during this time that a very unusual man came to our church. He had been a Word of Faith pastor for years but for some reason, which was never disclosed to me, he had left the ministry and was now living like a vagabond. He wasn't homeless, but he drove a car owned by someone else and he received financial support from somewhere unknown to me. From what I could tell, he just drifted. I found out rather quickly that he didn't stay very long at any place. At the onset of our relationship, he went as far as to tell me that he would only be here a few months then he would be gone forever. This proved to be true.

Having said all of this, I want you to know that he was a difficult man to say the least. He was controlling and demanding. To be honest, I didn't appreciate this aspect of our relationship after the experiences I had in the past with such people. In the end, he violated my space too much and had to move on. After about five months we parted ways and in retrospect I was glad to see him go! To this day, I am thankful he was there, while at the same time, I am even more thankful that he was not there for a lengthy stay. I write that sentence with a smile on my face that only someone in my shoes would understand.

His short companionship in my life did have some tremendous blessings in the midst of the aggravation he created. During those months, he drove me to intense prayer and bible study. Raylene and I would meet him daily at the church for prayer and study throughout that season, which lasted from the end of Spring to early Fall. I know that we needed this time to snap our attention to the mission God placed in our hearts. If you will remember, I am fighting discouragement and even depression at this point as a result of the tumultuous transition going on in my ministry and the church I pastored.

I had not shared with him, Raylene, or my accountability pastors the constant drumbeat in my head that I had failed and that I may have missed God's will for my life. I was trying to ignore this, yet the voice inside me kept saying, "You're not supposed to be here! People put you here, not God."

This line of thinking had with it several scenarios that were driving me crazy. One of those was the possibility that the original voters had it wrong and I should have never taken the church after my father-in-law. I also thought that it was possible for the other set of voters to have it wrong, and we should have never left the denomination. I was confident in what God had directed me to do at both of those times but was now in question. What if all of this was man's work and not a work of God?

I will never forget the night that strange man busted past everyone else, stepped inside my office, and closed the door. He was obviously on a mission, and he looked extremely intense. His voice was in a low tone as he placed both hands on my desk and leaned forward towards me as I sat in my chair. "Do you believe that all life comes from God?" speaking intensely at me. I was stumped. There was no warning for this pop quiz! I had no context for which to bounce off this bizarre question.

Seeing my perplexity he asked again with more intensity, "Do you believe all life comes from God?" Bringing myself under composure I reflected quickly in my mind and said, "Yes. God is the giver of all life. Therefore, all life comes from God." He wasn't through as his next question burst out in the same low intensity, "Then how do you know it is the will of God for you to be alive?" I had just felt a tinge of "I passed the test" relief when I found myself sinking into the hole of perplexity again.

He just stared until I coughed up an answer, "Because I'm alive. I know it is the will of God for me to be alive because I am alive." I felt he was satisfied with my answer but then He rocked my world with a third and final question. Before turning to leave he asked, "How do you know it is God's will for you to pastor this church?" To me the answer was now clear. He was walking toward the door as I said, "It is God's will for me to pastor this church because I am pastoring this church."

I realized in a fresh way that I was following God's plan and he was still in charge! If God wanted something different, he would move me out of the way—especially since I am so open to his influence and direction. I had forgotten that people didn't make this happen. My wife's dad didn't do this. A vote from the people didn't do this. God was sovereign enough to get us here and he was sovereign enough to keep us here or to move us out of the way!

This is God's doing. God is the source and God will make this thing happen in his timing and perfect plan. This is the driving force behind David's words in Psalm 27:12-14.

> Psalm 27:12–14 (NIV84) Do not turn me over to the desire of my foes, for false witnesses rise up against me, breathing out violence. I am still confident of this: I will see the goodness of the Lord in the land of the living. Wait for the Lord; be strong and take heart and wait for the Lord.

David was a man who understood adversity and the need for resources. He stood firm in the midst of everything he was facing and declared that the Source was coming! He had confidence in the fact that he would live to see the help and blessing of the Lord in the midst of adversity. In other words, he declared, "I'm going to live to say, God did that!"

He lived in such a way as to expect to see God's blessing in his present life. He didn't grow nostalgic thinking about what God had already done and he didn't live on a vague hope of what God is going to do at some point in the future. He remained thankful for blessings past, hopeful for blessings future, and expectant for blessings present. The land of the living is the present and David expected to see something happen in it. That expectancy gave him the faith to persevere until he saw it come to pass.

Let me pause for a moment to say that we must not forget that there are certain principles that apply in the Grace Life. One of these principles is the fact that we must hold onto our faith in present resources until we see God send the resources we need for the ultimate victory. David understood this. Reading his story is a roller coaster ride of victory and defeat. He experienced triumph and at times, tragedy. But he knew how to hold on!

For him, to wait on the Lord did not mean to sit in the corner and suck your thumb. His idea of waiting was to hear the word of the Lord and keep moving in the right direction. While waiting for the final answer, he fulfilled God's purpose in the moment! He then said, "God did that."

The key to this kind of faith is to never lose sight of the present blessing while you are waiting on the ultimate answer. Even though you may not have seen the answer you are looking for, you are still surrounded by the blessings of God. David's example can teach us the valuable lesson to never ignore the blessings in the moment while waiting on the future blessings to come.

To me, one of the most important concepts concerning holding on to faith is to act upon those things that the Holy Spirit is calling you to do in that moment. Our faith needs to catapult us into knowing, *"God did that so that I can do this."* At the heart of this concept is the idea that our actions position us for the miraculous blessing. These actions are the Grace Works that accompany the Grace Life.

Looking back at David's example, if he had quit during the trying times, he would have never seen the miraculous blessing that came later. His understanding of waiting on the Lord led him to do what he knew God was calling him to do at this point while standing firm in his faith for the ultimate answer. This was accomplished because he understood the difference between resources and the Source. The times when he did not have the resources to win, he rested his faith on the fact that the Source was still with him.

This way of living was even exampled in David's first foray into the public spotlight. He was delivering food to his brothers on the battlefield and discovered that the entire army of Israel, including King Saul, was paralyzed in fear of a loud-mouthed Giant. You will remember this story as the infamous David and Goliath incident found in 1 Samuel 17.

When David arrived on the scene it was clear that everyone was looking at the resources they had at their disposal and thinking they were the source. Even Saul, who was anointed by God, made the decision that they could not beat this giant because they lacked the resources needed for victory. The entire army was shaking with fear over one man who happened to be freakishly big!

Their fear was based on the mentality that their "source" was limited. They had limited weapons, limited skill, limited strength, limited size, and limited faith! When David arrived, they discovered rather quickly that his understanding was on a different level.

> 1 Samuel 17:32–37 (NIV84)—David said to Saul, "Let no one lose heart on account of this Philistine; your servant will go and fight him." Saul replied, "You are not able to go out against this Philistine and fight him; you are only a boy, and he has been a fighting man from his youth." But David said to Saul, "Your servant has been keeping his father's sheep. When a lion or a bear came and carried off a sheep from the flock, I went after it, struck it and rescued the sheep from its mouth. When it turned on me, I seized it by its hair, struck it and killed it. Your servant has killed both the lion and the bear; this uncircumcised Philistine will be like one of them, because he has defied the armies of the living God. The Lord who delivered me from the paw of the lion and the paw of the bear will deliver me from the hand of this Philistine." Saul said to David, "Go, and the Lord be with you."

David's focus was not on the resources that surrounded him! His focus was on the Source! His experience proved that it is God's strength and God's ability working through us that makes the difference! *God did that so that I can do this!* David literally said, "God did that so I killed the lion and the bear! God did that so I am a conqueror! And I will beat this giant because God is my source! Everything else is simply the resource available to me to get God's job done!"

His idea of waiting on the Lord was saying to Saul that he would go fight the giant. Waiting to him meant picking up stones, which were a *resource*. Waiting meant walking out to meet the giant. Walking was a *resource*. Waiting meant putting a stone in the sling, which again was a *resource*. To him, waiting meant using the sling and releasing the stone, both are *resources*.

Then we find the stone striking the giant in the exact spot to knock him down and at this point we see the *Source* come into view! To David, waiting on the Lord meant running to the fallen giant and using the giant's sword to cut off his head. These are *resource* actions. In the end he declared, "God did that!" The *Source* gave him the strength, courage, faith, tools, and tenacity to do God's work.

It is important to see that God brought the victory by giving David all of the necessary resources needed for that victory at the exact time he would need them. He never had to question whether or not he would have what he needed to win. His confidence was in a God who would not fail him at the crucial moments. The Source provided the resources, and David used them to win the battle.

We must not forget that the resources would have held no value if David had not of acted upon them in faith. Giants don't fall by themselves. Someone from the winning team has to step up and take on the challenge by faith. While everyone else in the army of Israel was focused on the limited resources they had at their disposal and their perceived inability to beat the giant, David used even less resources while staying focused on the ability of the unlimited Source.

History shows that David won the battle because of his faith in the Source and not because of his own ability or strength. David's response to Goliath reveals this intent.

> 1 Samuel 17:45–47 (NIV84)—David said to the Philistine, "You come against me with sword and spear and javelin, but I come against you in the name of the Lord Almighty, the God of the armies of Israel, whom you have defied. This day the Lord will hand you over to me, and I'll strike you down and cut off your head. Today I will give the carcasses of the Philistine army to the birds of the air and the beasts of the earth, and the whole world will know that there is a God in Israel. All those gathered here will know that it is not by sword or spear that the Lord saves; for the battle is the Lord's, and he will give all of you into our hands."

Although David would use the sling, toss the stone, and ultimately use the giant's sword to severe his head, he still gave all of the credit for the upcoming victory to God. He understood what was really happening. Instead of declaring his own ability to fight or the strength of his weapons and instruments of warfare as the source of the victory, he remained steadfastly focused on the Source.

There is a tremendous lesson to be learned here when it comes to living the Grace Life. One of the easiest things to do is to focus and rely on the resources around us and to lose sight of the fact that God is the Source and the victory is only won through him. This speaks right to the human tendency to desire self-reliance and shows us that we must become very intentional in our faith. It is obvious that the giant came with resources as well—sword, spear, javelin, experience, ability, and size—but David came with resources and the Source! This is the difference maker. His ultimate testimony was, "God did that so that I can do this!"

Another lesson learned in this exchange is that although it is very true that we must never confuse resources with the Source, we must be willing to act upon the resources provided to us by him. Abraham, who is the father of faith, understood this reality. He not only heard the promise; he acted upon the promise. God told him to leave everything he knew behind and walk around what would be the possessed Promised Land, so he walked! God told him to offer his son as a sacrifice, and he did so willingly. This occurrence is used as an expression of the powerful combination of faith and action in James 2:21-24.

> James 2:21–24 (NIV84)—Was not our ancestor Abraham considered righteous for what he did when he offered his son Isaac on the altar? You see that his faith and his actions were working together, and his faith was made complete by

what he did. And the scripture was fulfilled that says, "Abraham believed God, and it was credited to him as righteousness," and he was called God's friend. You see that a person is justified by what he does and not by faith alone.

Faith and action work together to fulfill God's purpose on the Earth! Keep in mind that these actions are not what we do to earn God's favor; they are the byproducts of God's favor, influence, and power working in our lives. Action on our part should always be a result of Kingdom Advance in our lives and not an act of attempting to earn a place in it. As the Holy Spirit opens to us the potential, we move out and possess. This is truly what the Grace Life is all about.

The examples of both David and Abraham show us that our lives are to be a combination of faith and action if we are going to accomplish Kingdom purpose! We have divine favor, divine influence, and divine power so that we can be effective, functioning members of the Kingdom of God while at the same time having full assurance of our salvation in Christ.

God is highly interested in us exercising our faith through Grace Works. I remember the first time I understood in my spirit the words, "Exercise your faith." In 1990, I was preaching in Zealand, New Brunswick, Canada. In that church there was a young lady who had been born with a debilitating spinal problem. As she matured, her spine did not grow in the same proportion as the rest of her body. Consequently, she was stooped over and barely able to function.

We had witnessed some miracles in that series of services and her faith was soaring that God would give her a particular request. Due to her condition, she was unable to lift her arms to put her hands over her head. As I would discover, she had been praying for the ability to lift her hands high enough to fix her own hair. One night, as the time of prayer at the end of the service was progressing, the ladies were praying with her in the altar area at the front of the auditorium.

They had positioned themselves in a circle around this girl and asked if I would come pray with her for this miracle. As I stepped into the area, the Holy Spirit spoke to me to tell her to exercise her faith. I turned to the pastor's wife and asked her to convey this message to the young lady even though I really wasn't sure what the full extent of this statement was. What I did know was this girl needed to break through the walls of fear that had her bound.

As we continued to pray and worship, it became clear to me that if this girl was going to experience a miracle she needed to stop being afraid to let go in free worship. I felt she needed to break forth in a joyful dance like David did in the Old Testament or like the lame man did in the third chapter of Acts. By doing this she would know that God had given her the request. I knew that she did not need to worship freely to earn the miracle; she needed to break free of doubt and fear by worshipping freely as a result of the miracle.

The problem was that she was afraid of losing her balance and would not loosen up. Looking back on this night I believe that she had already been given the miracle but was so tense with fear that she didn't know it! I continued to ask the pastor's wife encourage her to just loosen up and worship the Lord. She also reminded her that there were plenty of ladies around her and they would not let her fall or get hurt. All of a sudden, this girl let go. She began to rock back and forth and lift her foot off of the ground.

At this point, all of the fear left as the joy of the Lord became her strength. She didn't care what she looked like or acted like! She simply began to exercise her faith by rejoicing in the Lord. The most amazing thing happened as she rocked back and forth worshipping, her hands shot up over her head in praise! The whole place lit up in demonstrative worship as his young lady led the dance troupe. It was as though her breaking free from the bondage of fear caused everyone to break free of whatever they were bound with.

She was no longer worried about falling, and she freely moved around with her hands in the air, rejoicing in the presence of God. The vital point is that she was able to do this as a result of the touch of the Holy Spirit that night. She danced because God did that! She lifted her hands because God did that. I witnessed the exercising of her faith, as her actions combined with her faith became the vehicle for the miraculous. After service she was sitting on the pew showing everyone how that she, for the first time in her life, could adjust the clip in her hair by herself. God did that too.

A couple of weeks later she met me in the hallway at a conference I was preaching nearby. She asked me if I liked her hair. She then said, "I fixed it all by myself!"

That was a first again. How could you not like it? God did that! She faced her giant by putting action with her faith and God brought that giant down. Through the years, I have come to appreciate the "exercise your faith" mentality that God revealed to me that night.

For me, there are two powerful connotations to it. First, just as someone exercises his or her authority, we need to not be afraid to act in the authority of our faith. Authority has no value if it is not exercised through action. This is what makes great leaders—they know when they need to step up and do something. The same is true with faith. When we exercise our faith, we are acting on what faith is declaring in our lives and we do the things that the Holy Spirit is calling us to do.

The second connotation to "exercise your faith" is much like that of an athlete. Through exercise, athletes are able to accomplish difficult tasks. In fact, exercise is the vial component that keeps many people from physical accomplishments. Whether it is lifting weights, walking, or running a marathon, exercise brings strength, stamina, and vitality. This is also true with faith. The more faith is used the stronger it becomes. People who exercise their faith become strong in Kingdom Advance.

In both sceneries, action on the part of the one having faith is required. For the girl in New Brunswick, God had given her the authority and the strength to raise her hands above her head; she simply needed to exercise it! Exercising her faith meant to worship as though her physical impairment wasn't there. She took authority over the fear and yielded to the Holy Spirit's influence in demonstrative worship.

I close this chapter with an encouraging admonishment, let's face our giants and possess our Promised Lands! Don't be afraid to move out and exercise your faith. What is God calling you to do right now? How is grace influencing you to move? Do it! God has already given you everything you need for success. The authority and strength of your faith is already present, so exercise it! *God did that so that I can do this!*

Chapter Eight

FAITH AND ACTION

The understanding covered in the last chapter is vital if we are going to be everything God has called us to be. The foundation that I laid for the continuing concept is that God is the source of everything good and perfect and that everything else is the resource he has provided for our use. It is also true that faith in action produces fruit for the Kingdom of God and is the avenue by which God blesses us as individuals.

One of the greatest hindrances to Kingdom productivity is the idea that the action of Grace Works in our lives is legalism on our part. As James wrote, faith and action are working together not working against each other. Paul gave an interesting summary about faith in action in 1 Thessalonians 1:3.

> 1 Thessalonians 1:3 (NIV84)—We continually remember before our God and Father your work produced by faith, your labor prompted by love, and your endurance inspired by hope in our Lord Jesus Christ.

Ponder this text for a moment. Paul was actually giving thanks to God for their work produced by faith, their labor prompted by love, and their endurance inspired by hope. These words are a prime example of the church being commended because they were operating with both faith and action. This church was not passively sitting by waiting on the return of the Lord. They were fully functioning under grace to do Kingdom stuff. God was up to stuff and so were they!

God gave them the resources and they were faithful to administer them through their work, labor, and endurance. In this same way, our faith should mobilize us into doing something with the resources God has provided. This is what living the Grace Life and operating in Grace Works is all about!

An important understanding is that all resources come from God in order for us to have the opportunity to act upon grace and faith to advance the Kingdom through Grace Works. It is here that we really start living in this manner: *GOD DID THAT SO THAT I CAN ACT UPON IT AND DO THIS!*

We must be careful to remember that those actions on our part, combined with grace and faith, not only propagate the Kingdom of God they also position us for miraculous provision. This truth is evident from the salvation experience that is the beginning of all things Christian in our lives. Romans 10:8-10 shows the dynamic combination of faith and action.

> Romans 10:8–10 (NIV84)—But what does it say? "The word is near you; it is in your mouth and in your heart," that is, the word of faith we are proclaiming: That if you confess with your mouth, "Jesus is Lord," and believe in your heart

that God raised him from the dead, you will be saved. For it is with your heart that you believe and are justified, and it is with your mouth that you confess and are saved.

In these verses we discover that salvation comes as a result of the actions defined as "believe and confess." This shows how deeply important the combination of faith and action is. It is not enough to just believe. Both believing and confessing (faith and action) bring the salvation needed for the new birth experience. Once this principle is understood, one can clearly see that a miraculous blessing follows. Believe plus confess equals salvation in the same way that faith and action equal Kingdom productivity. The Grace Life is a life of blessed action!

Our faith needs to explode into a revelation that God wants each one of us to be in a position of blessing in order for the Kingdom of God to be blessed through us. Each believer should be able to look back in their lives and see work produced by faith and labor prompted by love with Kingdom fruit evident. We have each been saved for action, not inaction! We have been called for activity not inactivity! There is a corresponding action that should accompany our faith in every circumstance! James hit this point hard in James 2:14-18.

> James 2:14–18 (NIV84)—What good is it, my brothers, if a man claims to have faith but has no deeds? Can such faith save him? Suppose a brother or sister is without clothes and daily food. If one of you says to him, "Go, I wish you

well; keep warm and well fed," but does nothing about his physical needs, what good is it? In the same way, faith by itself, if it is not accompanied by action, is dead. But someone will say, "You have faith; I have deeds." Show me your faith without deeds, and I will show you my faith by what I do.

Those really are strong words—faith that is not accompanied by action is dead! The response for many at this point is to start crying foul. They excuse any need for works by declaring works are legalism. Well to be straight, they can be. If you think what you are doing is earning brownie points with God, then it is legalism. If you think your salvation is based on how well you perform, then it is legalism. If you think God likes you more as a result of the works you do, then it is legalism.

The balance for us is to understand that our works do not earn grace; on the contrary, these works are actions that take place as the result of grace. The negative mentality concerning works that we must overcome is that grace and faith do not cancel out works on our part. Action accompanies grace and faith as a product of them! The point is that God did that so that I can do this. That is the Grace Life! The Church at Philippi must have understood this principle for Paul to address this in Philippians 4:14-19.

Philippians 4:14–19 (niv84)—Yet it was good of you to share in my troubles. Moreover, as you Philippians know, in the early days of your acquaintance with the gospel, when I set out from Macedonia, not one church shared with me in the matter of giving and receiving, except you only; for even when I was in Thessalonica, you sent me aid again and again when I was in need. Not that I am looking for a gift, but I am looking for what may be credited to your account. I have received full payment and even more; I am amply supplied, now that I have received from Epaphroditus the gifts you sent. They are a fragrant offering, an acceptable sacrifice, pleasing to God. And my God will meet all your needs according to his glorious riches in Christ Jesus.

They got it! They understood that God, as the Source, gave the resources in their lives to them. They should then steward them in such a way as to advance his Kingdom through Grace Works. Here is the progression: God gave them the resources, they acted upon the prompting of the Holy Spirit to sow those resources into the Kingdom work done by Paul, and then miraculous provision was promised to come back to them. Paul literally said that God would supply all of their need according to his glorious riches! What a thought. The one who is the source of all things good is now taking personal responsibility to supply the needs of those who live the Grace Life and act on their faith.

What is interesting to me is that even in the early church there were people who lost sight of this principle or did not understand it in the first place! This must be true since Paul said to the Philippians that they were the only ones that understood and acted upon their faith in this manner! I say thank God someone did! I find myself saying to the Church at Philippi, "Give me an example to follow!" This demonstrates that people of faith and action live for Kingdom Advance and the church of Philippi did in a marvelous way.

Kingdom advancers act on their faith and pray. They act on their faith and move toward the goal. They act on their faith and give generously of their finances. They act on their faith and worship. Kingdom advancers act on their faith and witness. Kingdom Advance is propagated through the lives of people who are willing to take action as the Holy Spirit directs. Someone has to be willing to step out on faith and face the giant.

I find myself asking those who oppose Grace Works, "What good is having the resources if you are not willing to use them because of being afraid of (or having a misconception of) works?" Over and over again I have seen people who were so afraid of doing the wrong thing that they failed at doing the right thing. There have been times that I've been that person as well, so I'm not throwing stones. We cannot take "go" out of the gospel nor can we be negligent to act when the Holy Spirit directs.

I am thankful that that there have been times when I did get it. I took that challenge during my first solo pastorate at a small church in Oklahoma City, Oklahoma. I was just coming off of a three-year stint as the associate pastor at the church my father-in-law pastored in south Tulsa, Oklahoma. To say the least, I was eager to fly out on my own with my Lead Pastor wings and jumped at the opportunity that was made available to me at that time.

The church I was to take with this new ministry assignment had been locked in a stale and diminishing pattern for many years. When I got there, there were about thirty people who were mostly over forty and a handful of young people associated with them. What I realized immediately was that there was no life at all in the spirit of this church's membership. Even the casual observer would recognize that this church was dying.

In an attempt to give you a quick picture of how it was, let me say that they didn't even have functioning classrooms for children. It was a mess. There were two levels in the church building. The main auditorium filled most of the top floor and a small kitchen, fellowship area, and classrooms were situated in the downstairs basement. Walking into the dungeon-like environment downstairs, you would discover that all but two of the classrooms were filled to the ceiling with junk and were not functional. Literally, filled with junk.

What had happened here was tragic. The pastor that was there before me loved to barter at swap meets and garage sales as a hobby and would use his skills to generate extra income. The result of his weekly forays into these buying and trading opportunities, mixed with the lack of vision for growth in the congregation, was evident throughout the basement of this church. As the rooms were not being used for ministry, he would store his extra finds in them. Over the course of time, most of the rooms were filled to capacity. They were full of junk that was waiting to be bartered or sold on one of his swapping adventures. For whatever reason, when he left from pastoring the church, he left all of this stuff for us to deal with. You literally had to climb on top of this stuff to get into the rooms.

There were two functioning classrooms downstairs, one was used by the handful of youth who were mostly siblings from one family, and the other was used for whatever child might possibly show up to any given service. Looking at the dates that were on the decorations on the walls, it was obvious that this room had not been used in a really long time. The newest decorations I remember seeing dated three years before our arrival as pastor.

I brought my wife and my two-year-old son, who was now the only child to speak of in the church, into this environment. The first thing on my agenda was to start preaching faith and vision to these people. Most of them caught on quickly and began to feel life being breathed into the church. The others just complained and were unsettled by the revitalization that was taking place. I have always found that to be one of the most interesting things about church life. Some people are so disconnected from the Grace Life that they oppose change even when it is God inspired and Kingdom advancing. This is especially true as some people get older.

It seems that if we are not careful we can get to a point where we don't care if there is anything to pass on to the next generation as long as nothing changes while we are alive. I really don't want to bog down here, so let me just cut to the chase: Don't be that person!

Be a world changer with your faith and action all the way through your Christian journey. Get connected with the generations that follow you and ensure that they have what they need to continue forward with the vision! Kingdom Advancers seek to empower the next generation and they make plans to pass something dynamic down to them.

Getting back to our story, we began to institute change in that church because something had to change and someone had to participate in it. We had no choice! If we had left it like it was, it would have died. We made up our minds to facilitate change even though the changes were unsettling to some long time members of the congregation.

Of note, and one thing that I have failed to mention, the founding pastor of that church, who had been in retirement for more than a decade, was still a member there. Someone would pick him up at the senior living center every week and bring him to church. Looking back I remember him being the most excited person in the church about the changes that were taking place. He knew in his heart that change was good and life was coming back to the church that he had spent most of his life supporting.

As I looked at everything that needed to be done, I knew one of the starting points was to do something in that downstairs, junk filled, dungeon of a basement. In a moment of faith, I called a church cleanout day. To my surprise, most of the people showed up. Trip after trip we went to the curb with armfuls of junk, old desks, lamps, car parts, bed frames, and too much other stuff to even mention. As the day progressed, Sunday school classrooms started to emerge. Making the most of this moment, I began to speak children into those classrooms!

We also doubled the size of the youth room by taking out a wall. I will never forget how much fun it was watching the teenage boys jump through those walls to make the holes in the sheetrock that we needed for demolition. That day we opened up the entire basement floor of the church for functioning use by piling the junk on the curb as trash. Did it anger a person or two? Yes. Did I care at that moment? No. We had resolved ourselves to being Spirit led and the Grace Life was in full swing whether we understood it or not.

What happened next was nothing short of amazing. As we were cleaning, I began to assign teachers for the classes that did not previously exist. Dividing the rooms by age classifications, I told the newly appointed teachers that they would be teaching the next Sunday and that they needed to get busy with decorating and studying the lessons. The surprised response was somewhat humorous as they reminded me that we only had one child in attendance and they didn't understand why having multiple classrooms ready in one week would be necessary. My response to that was to declare they would begin by teaching empty chairs until the kids came.

I was determined that we would have a functioning children's ministry the next week with or without kids. In my heart I understood that the key to unlocking the potential was to prepare the rooms before the kids came and not to wait on the kids to come before action was taken. What they needed was faith and action working together in their present situation to produce Kingdom results! God had already given the word.

It wasn't that these people didn't have the resources to make it happen, they didn't have the vision or the necessary action to make it happen. Without a vision there was no action and without action the church was dying. We are instructed in James 1:22 concerning how action accompanies faith.

> James 1:22 (NIV84)—Do not merely listen to the word, and so deceive yourselves. Do what it says.

The Grace Life produces the kind of people that hear the word and do what is says. True faith is being willing to do something with the word that has been given to you rather than passively sitting by in a state of lethargy. Too many times people want to hear the word but they don't want to do what it is saying. We decided to do something in that church!

Someone needed to wake up the people and help them realize that not only do we have everything we need to succeed we also have to be willing to do something with what we've got. They had the resources; they just didn't have a corresponding action. To our amazement, the next Sunday there were kids in every classroom including new young people in the enlarged youth room. None of the teachers ever taught empty chairs in those rooms that had not been used for several years.

We only pastored there seven months when we were called back to the church in south Tulsa to take the Lead Pastor position. In those seven months, the church that was dying more than doubled in size. We left that church in the middle of its third remodel project in the attempt to make room for more! The pastor that followed us continued on the same path and witnessed God's blessing. Faith and action on the part of the people produced Kingdom Advance. God did that so that I can do this!

We could have left things like they were. The reality is, that church would have died if it had continued on its path of doubt, fear, and inaction. Something had to happen in the minds of the people that convinced them to move in the same sense that we all must be movers! To stop the work of God, the enemy of the Kingdom doesn't have to take you out completely—all he has to do is convince you not to act.

There would have never been any kids to teach in those rooms as long as the rooms were unusable and the people did not have the mindset to work. The very week we made the rooms functional and had teachers in place to teach, we had kids! When we made room for growth, growth happened. It works that way because God is more interested in Kingdom Advance than we are. God is looking for willing participants.

The Grace Life teaches us that faith should have with it a corresponding action. The message reiterated throughout scripture is that the action part of faith is required for productivity. This is clear even in the Great Commission in Matthew 28:18-20.

> Matthew 28:18–20 (niv84)—Then Jesus came to them and said, "All authority in heaven and on earth has been given to me. Therefore go and make disciples of all nations, baptizing them in the name of the Father and of the Son and of the Holy Spirit, and teaching them to obey everything I have commanded you. And surely I am with you always, to the very end of the age."

The Great Commission is a commissioning for action with words such as go, make, baptizing, and teaching. These are all action words. The act of making disciples falls on those who have faith in the absolute authority of Jesus Christ and are willing to go, baptize, and teach. Disciples are not made by accident. Disciples are made through the combination of faith and action on the part of the believers.

A church that is immobile is not any better than having no church at all. Christians who will not mobilize into action are no different on the landscape of this world than if there were no Christian presence at all. It would be the same thing as having a police force that refuses to fight crime. They have the uniform and the badge. They have the patrol cars, the handcuffs, and the weapons. But they if they refuse to come out of the police station and go to work then all of their resources are of no value. It would only take a day or two for mayhem to break out in society under that paradigm.

It's also akin to having an army that refuses to prepare for combat, load its weapons, and go to battle. They may have all the resources to win the war, but if they don't show up to the fight they have lost by default. I sometimes wonder how much we are losing by default simply because we are not acting upon our faith. There is no use in having abundant resources if we are not willing to put them into action for Kingdom Advance.

I believe that many Christians have lost their Kingdom productivity as a result of being convinced that Grace Works are unnecessary and somehow anti-grace. The fear of self-works has paralyzed them into no works. We would be hard pressed to reconcile an anti-works theology with a bible that is full of action on the part of God's people. In a scriptural sense, action on the part of the believer is a natural outflow of the faith he or she declares.

Many times we end up living like paupers in the midst of God's riches because of this. While growing up in Humble, Texas we would make the trek to my grandparents house in Conroe, Texas multiple times a month. Our thirty-minute route to Conroe took us by a certain wooded corner just north of the San Jacinto River at Sorters Road and Highway 59. On this corner, lived a man who was a homeless squatter. He lived with no electricity, no running water, and seemingly no provisions.

His house (if you'd call it that) was a makeshift structure of scraps he had accumulated. We would often see him milling around outside of his shack, poking at the ground, and talking to himself. Looking at his chosen living conditions, it was evident that he was a recluse and a lonely pauper. Or so it seemed that he was a pauper.

At some point, someone began to miss seeing him and called the police to check it out. The police found that this man had died in his shack of scrap wood and tin. What came next was the surprise. According to the reports at the time, his remains were not all they found on that small patch of ground. It was reported that this man's mattress was stuffed full of money—hundred dollar bills kind of money! He had literally replaced all of the foam in the mattress with money.

As they explored further, they found hundreds of Mason Jars buried inside and outside of the shack. These jars were stuffed full of money just like the bed. This man could have lived a comfortable life with the resources he had at his disposal, but instead he hoarded the money and took it out of circulation. He was a pauper, not by resources but by his inability to act on those resources.

This story has been repeated many times throughout history. We have all heard stories like this of people who live far below their means simply because they have become immobilized by whatever circumstances have taken place in their lives. I feel the need to tell you that we have everything we need to advance the Kingdom. Don't bury the resources through inaction. Kingdom Advance requires faith and action on our part!

"Get up!" I can still hear my dad saying those words. "Get up, it's time to get ready."

My dad was always up before everyone else. He'd get up early to sit at the table, drink his coffee, and doodle neat designs on a piece of paper. When I was in school he was usually gone long before I was to get up, leaving the wake up call to my mom. After I graduated from school, I began working for the church. At this point, my dad would usually be the one to get me up before he left for his day. In his kind way he'd simple say, "Get up, it's time to get ready."

I'm saying that to all of us—get up! If there is to be Kingdom Advance we've got to get up and get moving. It is very important for us to not let the fear of legalism paralyze us into inactivity for Kingdom purpose. Get up and do something! I feel the need to remind us all that we need to stop sleeping on or burying our blessing and letting its benefits pass away by default. The church was never commanded to be immobile because of grace.

Grace is a mobilizer not an excuse for inactivity. The very essence of that Great Commission in Matthew 28 is contingent on the declaration for us to, "Go." It really doesn't get any plainer than that. We belong to a moving community of believers—at least that is how it is supposed to be. Kingdom Advance is waiting for the combination faith and action on our part! It really is that simple. We must never forget that the Grace Life is a life of blessed action! Can you hear in your spirit, "Get up, it's time to get ready!" *God did that so that I can do this!*

Chapter Nine

THE GRACE LIFE CYCLE

As discussed in the previous chapter, Abraham's faith and action were working together for Kingdom purpose according to James 2:22. This pivotal understanding will change your life if you will let it. I want to be bold in this moment by saying we need to stop making excuses for why we don't act for Kingdom purpose. It's time to let our faith explode into fruit bearing action!

Grace is steering us towards accomplishment because Kingdom advancement is the top priority of heaven. This was exampled clearly through the Old Testament, heralded loudly through the earthly life and ministry of Jesus Christ, and propagated widely throughout the New Testament church. God's favor, influence, and power are moving us to move for him!

This leads to the understanding that God did that so that I can do this. The heart of this has led me to believe that God is continually looking to pour resources on those who act upon their faith. This combination of faith and action is the epitome of faith that pleases God according to Hebrews 11:6.

> Hebrews 11:6 (NIV84)—And without faith it is impossible to please God, because anyone who comes to him must believe that he exists and that he rewards those who earnestly seek him.

If you cannot see in that verse that the two components of faith and action are producing miraculous provision, then you must not want to see it. Clearly the writer declares we must believe that God exists *and* that he rewards those who earnestly seek him. One more time we see that faith and action become a powerful combination in the Grace Life. On top of that, it is easy to earnestly seek God when you are infused with the reality that he is the Source, everything else is the resource, and he rewards those who act on their faith. It is a scriptural fact that through seeking there is reward.

What many people fail to understand is that a valuable component of seeking is found in the faith action of giving from the resources God has provided. When you do understand this, you don't find excuses not to give of your time, talent, and treasure. One of my favorite ways to explain this is the message of Seed Faith. Through the years, I have seen the blessing of God unleashed in my life as a result of practicing Seed Faith with my time, talent, and treasure.

It is important to begin any dialog concerning Seed Faith with the understanding that one must never think of Seed Faith as a gimmick to raise money for greedy gain or to pressure people into volunteer help. Seed Faith is a scriptural principle, established by God, used to bless those who sow into the Kingdom by faith.

The term, "Seed Faith" is simply used to describe God's principle of sowing and reaping of the seed in your life.

I must be clear in saying that where you put your seed is important. Sowing opportunities surround us all whether we recognize them as such or not. Even the act of paying the necessary bills for living is a sowing opportunity. For instance, we sow finances by paying for electricity and reap the benefit of lights and working electrical outlets. What I find amazing is how people don't mind putting their time, talent, and treasure into everything else but then complain about giving back to God through sowing into church life and Kingdom purpose.

We need to break the spiritual bondage of Kingdom stinginess! We all need a fresh zeal for prioritizing Kingdom business in our sowing. I have discovered that when we do not sow into Kingdom purpose it thwarts God's ultimate blessing in our lives. This principle of sowing and reaping was established clearly with the covenant God made with Noah in Genesis 8:22.

> Genesis 8:22 (NIV84)—"As long as the earth endures, seedtime and harvest, cold and heat, summer and winter, day and night will never cease."

Seedtime and harvest will not cease as long as the Earth is here. But keep in mind that this is not just an earth promise; it is a Kingdom promise. The awesome thing about this is that the seed that produces Kingdom harvest also produces more seed in your life. This is the Grace Life Cycle and it is evidenced throughout God's creation.

Going back to the understanding of Source and resource, everything we have belongs to God anyway! In reality, we operate with God's time, God's talent, and God's treasure. This means that we are the stewards of the resources he provides and that nothing else is the provider. It is a divine imperative that we take our place as manager and respect God's place as owner of all good and perfect things. We do this by demonstrating a willingness to give of the resources he has provided and use his provision in our life for Kingdom Advance.

What we tend to forget is that as the Source, he knows how to reward those who seek him with the resources he provides. I call this the Grace Life Cycle. He gives, we give back to him, and then he gives more. It is here that you trust that God did that so that I can do this! What is incredible is that the Grace Life Cycle never stops! This cycle of faith, action, and provision is revealed in Luke 6:37-38.

> Luke 6:37–38 (niv84)—"Do not judge, and you will not be judged. Do not condemn, and you will not be condemned. Forgive, and you will be forgiven. Give, and it will be given to you. A good measure, pressed down, shaken together and running over, will be poured into your lap. For with the measure you use, it will be measured to you."

The first thing that we must wrap our minds around is that the cycle always begins with God. Too many times we tend to start with the resource instead of with the Source. In order to fully maximize the effect of the Grace Life we must always keep God in first priority. Otherwise, our faith tends to shift away from God and to the things and the people that surround us. Breaking down these verses, let's look at how the Grace Life Cycle works:

- God does not judge (*God did that*) so that I can be in a position of not judging (*so I can do this*). I don't judge (*I can do this*) therefore God does not judge (*God did that*).
- God does not condemn (*God did that*) so that I can be in a position of not condemning (*so I can do this*). I don't condemn (*I can do this*) therefore God does not condemn (*God did that*).
- God forgives (*God did that*) so that I can be in a position to forgive (*so that I can do this*). I forgive (*I can do this*) therefore God forgives (*God did that*).
- God gives (*God did that*) so that I can be in a position of giving (*so that I can do this*). I give (*I can do this*) therefore God gives (*God did that*).

The cycle begins with God, flows to me, flows through me, back to God, and then back to me—over and over again!

This moves into the realm of Seed Faith taking a functioning role in our lives! God is the source, he gives us the resource, and from that resource we give. We then find that this act of sowing by faith becomes the catalyst for more resources to be poured into our lap.

But it doesn't stop there. When we put action with our faith, the Source increases the resources in our lives! God does that with a good measure, pressed down, shaken together, and running over. His return always supersedes that which we have sown. Suddenly we realize that *God did that so that I can do this. Then God does that so that I can do more of this.*

When looking at the Grace Life Cycle in Luke 6:38 it looks like this: God gives (*God did that*) so that I can be in a position of giving (*so that I can do this*). God gives back in abundance through Seed Faith provision (*God did that*) so that I can continue to give (*so that I can do more of this*). Once again, God did that so that I can do this then God does that so that I can do more of this—and the Kingdom Advances!

If the church is going to advance the Kingdom of God in this world we must return to absolute faith in the reciprocal blessing tied to the act of Kingdom giving. God supplies and increases the seed in our lives in order for us to continue moving the Kingdom of God forward on the earth. This abundant supply is activated by faith and action, putting us in the stewardship role of the Grace Life Cycle. The same principle is found in 2 Corinthians 9:10-13.

> 2 Corinthians 9:10–13 (NIV84)—Now he who supplies seed to the sower and bread for food will also supply and increase your store of seed and will enlarge the harvest of your righteousness. You will be made rich in every way so that you can be generous on every occasion, and through us your generosity will result in thanksgiving to

God. This service that you perform is not only supplying the needs of God's people but is also overflowing in many expressions of thanks to God. Because of the service by which you have proved yourselves, men will praise God for the obedience that accompanies your confession of the gospel of Christ, and for your generosity in sharing with them and with everyone else.

I bring these verses back up because I want you to see the Grace Life Cycle that is evident here. This becomes very important because the Grace Life Cycle is how the Kingdom of God advances in the world. God supplies seed to the sower and bread for food (*God did that*). We are the sower who sows into the Kingdom harvest field (*so that I can do this*).

We then find that God increases our store of seed and enlarges the harvest (*God did that*) of our right actions (*so that I can do more of this*). There is a clear admonishment from Paul that in the area of giving these people acted on their faith by sowing finances into Kingdom Advance and the result was increased seed and provision—both in the Kingdom and in their personal lives.

Their actions produced the continued blessing of God as he increased their store of seed for enlarged harvests. He even said that it was obedience that accompanied their confession of faith! You may ask, "Obedience to what?" The answer is clear that it was obedience to the divine favor, influence, and power that was upon them. Their obedience was in taking faith and action to the high call of the Grace Life.

This is a tremendous insight for us in living the Grace Life! What we need to do is get in the flow! I have heard it said many times, "If God can get it through you, he will get it to you." Be one of those people. Stop letting the enemy steal your faith when it comes to being a sower. An overflowing blessing is coming your way.

This whole passage screams to us the reality that God, as the source, gives resources. When these resources are stewarded right, there is a blessing BOTH to the one giving and those to whom it was given. The cycle shows itself strong in the word of God and in your life. By this principle the Kingdom of God is advanced in the Earth! Faith and action produce Kingdom Advance and Kingdom blessings.

Don't buy into the lie that faith doesn't have corresponding action! Don't let anyone convince you that grace and works do not belong together. Don't listen to the voices around you that say God doesn't reward those who sow with an increase of seed in their lives. Live the Grace Life! Allow the favor, influence, and power of God to work in you and through you for Kingdom Advance. *God did that so that I can do this. Then God does that so that I can do more of this.*

Chapter Ten

LIVING ON FAITH AND FUMES

Too many times we find ourselves boxed in with our resources that seem limited. This is not living the Grace Life to its fullest potential. The Grace Life is about getting outside of our box and living in the unlimited resources that flow from the unlimited Source! Grace is working in us to enable us to be everything God is calling us to be. It is also giving us everything we need to do everything God is calling us to do.

This is a key understanding for Kingdom Advance. We cannot accomplish the task on our own, but we can more than accomplish the task through the grace of God. It is when we start thinking that we cannot do what God is calling us to do or we cannot give what God is influencing us to give that we are no longer living by grace. At that point we have begun to paint ourselves in the corner of doubt and lock ourselves in the box of our own strength and ability.

Let me be totally transparent in my next statement. I can't live for God without God! If you will be transparent as well, you will admit with me that none of us can. We might be able to follow a list of rules and recite dogma and creeds on our own, but that doesn't mean we are truly living for God. I have spent the last few years of my life running from the kind of religious experience that operates on rules rather than relationship. Many people have.

The Grace Life releases us from the box of self-sufficiency and puts us in harmonious relationship with the Father and his all sufficient nature. No longer do we have to rely on our own ability, strength, and resources. Because of this, we do not have to fear when God speaks to us to move out by faith. This is especially important when you consider the fact that fear is one of the greatest momentum killers of Kingdom Advance. This is why it is important for us to engrain 2 Corinthians 5:7 into our spirits.

> 2 Corinthians 5:7 (niv84)—We live by faith, not by sight.

Some translations use the word, "walk" instead of "live" for this verse. Either way we must understand that living the Grace Life is a life and walk of faith—not sight. The implication here is that this is a spiritual walk not a physical walk. The aspirations are not of the flesh but of the Spirit. What many people miss is the fact that although many of the resources are physical in nature they are spiritual in essence. It is here that we can get confused because sometimes we see the resources and sometimes we don't.

This is an important reason why our faith journey cannot be built on what we see or don't see in the natural. What we see in the natural is not all there is to it. The Grace Life declares that although we may not see it in the natural at this time it does not mean it is not present in the spiritual! On the flip side of that coin, although we may see something in the natural it doesn't mean that it is the right resource in the spiritual. At this point we begin the process of learning to rely on the Source and not hold too much confidence in the various resources that surround us.

On many occasions I have struggled with an attitude that relied on the resources in my life rather than focusing on the Source. Here goes that transparency thing again! I have thought that the friends, people, things, or circumstances that surrounded me would bring me what I needed to succeed. Time and time again I have found myself in a situation where these things were proven to be an unreliable answer. Yet, I still stand! God has shown me that no matter what, He is my source and I will make it by his design.

I remember one time in particular when I felt certain relationships were the key to my success in ministry. I was hanging out with the "big time" preachers kids (who were now preachers themselves) and felt that by building a network of social relationships I would find the answer I was looking for to accomplish my ministry goals. Coming from a home where my dad rarely went to church, this seemed like my way to the top of the denominations influence and social ladder. What I found out in the end was they were not going to help me in any way, shape, or form.

My true standing among them was ultimately revealed and these relationships for the most part ended with a sudden blow of reality on my part. Fact is, I was an outsider and would always be. My feelings were hurt when I discovered that I was never considered a part of their elite level. They didn't mind my participation in their lofty events as long as I understood my place was on the sideline.

Throughout this situation I discovered one thing I know for sure, God really likes me! He warned me that something was about to happen that would change the nature of these relationships. Two hours before a devastating phone conversation with one of these friends, my mother-in-law called to say that she had been in prayer and God told her to tell me it was his doing and I would be all right. She then instructed me to go pray for strength—I did immediately.

It was in that time of prayer that I received the phone call from that friend. In an instant I knew the true nature of these relationships because of some things that were said to me. I lost confidence in those friends that night and our relationships were altered. Although I was devastated at that time, I know now that I was relying too heavily on them! This needed to be revealed because they were influencing me away from God's direction on my life. I had to accept the fact that they were not my source—God is! Has it hit you yet that God is your source too? I hope your faith in this rises!

Little did I know at that time, that this one experience would be the first of several experiences that would prepare me for one of the most severe shifts in ministry a preacher can make—transitioning a ministry and a church away from a denomination while continuing to pastor in the same location. In every instance, my resolve had to be to completely rely on God as the source and not to focus on the resources that may or may not be available. The blessing of the Grace Life is in knowing we have a constant source for all things needed even when resources are walking away.

If you don't get anything else in this book, get this, "Stop looking for everything else to solve what only God can solve and to do what only God can do!" Live the Grace Life! Our faith must rest on God and not on things (or the lack of things). Let me take a moment to shift our attention to the first circumstance mentioned above: *What is not seen in the natural may be present in the spiritual.* This is the very definition of faith in Hebrews 11:1 in the NKJV.

> Hebrews 11:1 (NKJV)—Now faith is the substance of things hoped for, the evidence of things not seen.

Faith, as the tangible substance of things hoped for, stands in place of those things in the spiritual until they are realized in the natural/physical. Using the same concept for emphasis, faith, as the evidence, stands in the place of those things spiritually as proof of their existence until they are revealed in the natural/physical. As you can see, faith is the spiritual thing you hold onto until the physical thing comes to pass. The Grace Life gives you the ability to not be paralyzed by fear when all you have is faith and fumes!

I believe that all of us will have the opportunity to discover what it really means to live on faith and fumes in the Grace Life. I learned this concept while I was a young traveling preacher from the mid-1980s to 1995. I took off to "evangelize" in a Pentecostal denomination at the ripe age of nineteen. Before I dive in too deeply, I should explain, "evangelize" to those who may be unfamiliar with the term.

An evangelist evangelizes. You have no idea how hard it is for me not to put, "LOL" after that sentence. In those days, evangelists were travelling preachers who went from church to church in the denomination holding special revival meetings. These "revivals" were meant to stir up the spiritual passion among the members of the congregations and those who were without Christ. This would be similar to the ministries of Billy Graham or Joyce Myers except it was every week, in different churches individually, and not in arenas and stadiums.

It was not uncommon, especially in my later years of doing this, to have at least six church services every week where I was expected to sing, preach, and conduct altar services to pray for the people. What you need to understand is that it didn't start out that busy. I can remember having a weekend set, maybe another service on another day, and then the rest of the calendar just having blank days waiting to be filled in.

If there is anything I need you to get right here, an evangelist is sort of like a beggar holding a sign up. Instead of it saying, "Will Work for Food," it says in a proverbial sense, "Will Preach for Food." The bottom line was that if the calendar did not show scheduled services then the bills were not going to be paid—or so it seemed at the time.

In my former denomination, young evangelists didn't get paid very much. Most of the pastors felt like they are doing you a favor just giving you the opportunity to hone your preaching skills on their church. To a certain degree, I can understand that. Usually young evangelists aren't the best at preaching and they even have the potential to make a mess of things because of their inexperience.

As it was, there were some pastors who blessed me with opportunities that my skill level did not deserve at the time. Pastor Pair in Oklahoma, Pastor Battrell in Texas, and Pastor Dupree in Arkansas stand out in my memory as pastors willing to champion my early ministry endeavors. The upside to this story is that by the time my twenty-first birthday rolled around things had begun to take off—even though I still made very little money.

Very little money is an understatement. I was preaching for small churches that didn't have much money themselves. I will never forget the multiple revivals I held where it was stated up front that they could feed me and give me a warm bed (or couch) to sleep on, but they could not pay me. I never turned down a single meeting under this arrangement. It was literally a life of faith and fumes—faith that God would see me through with only fumes in the gas tank.

To be honest, the faith and fumes life is not as scary when you are in a fifty-mile radius of your mom and dad, but my meetings were rarely that close to the safety of home. It was not uncommon for me to cross state lines out of Texas on a three or four hundred-mile trek for a three-night meeting. I had enough gas to get there but not enough to get back home—with no promise that I would receive any financial help for the journey. But God said, "Go" and I stuck by that! I was living by faith and not by sight. I was living by faith and fumes to be exact.

I live with the testimony that I watched God come through time and time again. Once, not only was my gas tank empty, my battery blew up under the hood. I had no idea how I was getting out of that town and to the next destination. Within the hour, someone drove to the house where I was staying and said, "God told me to come over here and buy you a battery." How did they even know about that except by God's providence? They then gave me enough cash to go to my next revival meeting. I could truly say, "God did that."

We all need to understand that living the Grace Life doesn't mean that there won't be times of faith and fumes. What the Grace Life does mean is that our confidence is in God all the way through! I knew that I had heard from God and my confidence had to rest in faith that he would take care of me even when my gas tank was empty!

This same principle will follow you while you are on your Grace Life journey. The bible is full of it. Paul and Peter and Silas did not escape it. Their testimony was that no matter what, God will sustain you. Paul's words in Philippians 4:11-13 demonstrate this principle perfectly.

> Philippians 4:11–13 (niv84)—I am not saying
> this because I am in need, for I have learned to
> be content whatever the circumstances. I know
> what it is to be in need, and I know what it is to
> have plenty. I have learned the secret of being
> content in any and every situation, whether
> well fed or hungry, whether living in plenty or
> in want. I can do everything through him who
> gives me strength.

Paul learned to be content in every circumstance because he was living the Grace Life. He knew that no matter the circumstance, God was the source! The glimpse of hope for all of us is to realize that even Paul had faith and fumes moments—although not experienced literally as fumes in an empty gas tank. His Grace Life experience wasn't focused on the resources, or the times when there was an apparent lack of resources. His focus was on the Source, and his confidence remained high.

He knew that when he didn't see it in the physical, that did not mean God had forsaken him. Our faith has to be stronger than the vacillating feelings of discouragement and disappointment that come during difficult times. Open your eyes to the possibility that everything you need in the physical has already been provided in the spiritual. Paul's contentment remained because when he didn't see it, he saw it. And when he did see it, he saw it as the provision of God. That is living high in the Grace Life.

I drove to New Brunswick, Canada from Houston, Texas in the fall of 1989 on faith and fumes. I will never forget following Pastor Morehouse from a preacher's conference in Indianapolis, Indiana to Doaktown, New Brunswick, thinking, *This is a really long drive.* This Texas boy had never gone this far—and it was on faith and fumes. It would be winter before I'd return home. I ended up spending a lot of time up there in the cold north over the next months. It was nothing less than miraculous.

The same thing happened my first trip to California in the summer of 1990. Faith and fumes took me to Santa Ana, California, financial gates opened wide, and my evangelistic ministry was sustained for the rest of its tenure. I relate these experiences to you because you have to catch it if you are going to persevere in the Grace Life. Just because you don't see it in the physical/natural world doesn't mean that it isn't there by faith!

Answer the question, "Have I heard from God?" If you know for sure you have, I dare you to move! If God gives you the dream, he will resource it as well. The right people are coming! The finances are coming! The materials are coming! Faith is the substance of things hoped for.

The other circumstance mentioned earlier is: *Although a resource is seen in the natural, that doesn't mean it is the right resource for that moment in the spiritual.* This is not to say that we have to be afraid as to whether or not the good resource is for our use. It is simply admitting that there are times when multiple solutions may be present and we have to weigh our options as to what is best. There may be other times that the resources you do have are not right for the moment and you need to wait for God to provide something else.

No matter how you arrive at the conclusion, there are definite moments when what is available is not what is expedient for the particular situation at hand. You may have someone you can call. There may be a bank account you can empty out. You may be offered a new opportunity. Walking by faith takes the issue of resources to God in prayer and to wise counsel. I have discovered that sometimes it is better to wait on a word from God and another resource rather than to take matters into my own hands simply because I could make something happen with the resources already surrounding me.

I jump sometimes and sometimes I don't. When I see something that needs to be done, I usually go for it—unless I know it will be difficult to deal with and the long-term implications are severely negative. No matter what the circumstance or what level of insecurity I may feel, I know that I must eventually act, and sometimes I do that without thinking or even praying. I've done that with people, which is not the best thing to do. One thing I know for sure is that impulsive moves can be treacherous.

This is especially true if you are being influenced by an outside (or inside) source that is not God. It reminds me of a really bad move I once made in my early career as a pastor involving a young man who had been serving on our pastoral team as youth pastor. There had been some issues that needed to be addressed, and I had been slow in dealing with them—although the Holy Spirit had prompted me on several occasions to talk with him about them.

If I would have moved in one of those moments it would have gone much better than my later self propagated fiasco. Have you ever been there? Moving under the influence and power of grace is far better than moving on your own. I look back and wish I had moved when God said to move rather than waiting until that later self-induced moment.

In this instance, insubordination was high and another pastoral team member had his fill of it. In a moment of anger he approached me concerning his frustrations with this team member. His frustration motivated my frustration and that was the moment that I jumped! I jumped at the influence of a person rather than under the care of grace. As a result, I exemplified very little grace in the meeting.

Yes, I had all of the resources I needed to take care of it. I made my list. I had my proof of insubordination. My own ability to communicate effectively the problem at hand was at its peak. My courage was up and adrenalin was flowing. I also had the backing of the people that wielded the influence and support I needed to get the job done. That is all great, but what I did not have was the right grace provision to handle the issues that day. I also did not have the right timing. I ran on emotion, anger, and frustration and not on divine favor, influence, and power.

There it was. One hour before the biggest youth event ever planned by this young man, I called him in. I decided to just take care of this now, even though the resource of time and motive was wrong. I ended up demoralizing him by taking all of the excited air out of his ministry sails. He resigned just a few days later to leave the ministry all together. As far as I know, he has not returned to the call he felt so sure of before. It stands as one of my most remembered regrets in personal leadership moments.

What I know now is that the resources I had were wrong for the occasion. I should have and could have waited, but I didn't. I do not hold myself to blame for the young man's response and I did apologize to him more than once, but looking back I realize that I could have done a better job living the Grace Life in this situation. I should have gone to the young man earlier when the Holy Spirit was prompting me to talk to him, but I didn't. I should have waited that day when the Holy Spirit was telling me to wait, but I didn't. I charged head first into the fray and made a mess.

I fully understand today that just because I can do something doesn't mean I should do something. I can sense that David must have felt the same way on the day of his anointing debut before Israel. He understood the lion and the bear incidents as God's doing. Sure, it was David's awareness and David's hands, but David knew the real deal was in the fact that "God did that."

As you read the story, you can see that David discovered if you are not careful, in the midst of the circumstance, resources have a way of becoming a distraction. The pre-contest interview with King Saul almost knocked David off of his God focus that day. With David's confidence seemingly secure in God's direction, Saul reveals other resource options in 1 Samuel 17:37-40.

> 1 Samuel 17:37–40 (NIV84)—The Lord who delivered me from the paw of the lion and the paw of the bear will deliver me from the hand of this Philistine." Saul said to David, "Go, and the Lord be with you." Then Saul dressed David in his own tunic. He put a coat of armor on him and a bronze helmet on his head. David fastened on his sword over the tunic and tried walking around, because he was not used to them. "I cannot go in these," he said to Saul, "because I am not used to them." So he took them off. Then he took his staff in his hand, chose five smooth stones from the stream, put them in the pouch of his shepherd's bag and, with his sling in his hand, approached the Philistine.

The resources available to David in the company of the king were different than those he had when he was in the field alone with his father's sheep. Obviously, David was moved by the influence of King Saul. He was moved enough to try on the armor and pick up weapons that were made available by the king. As he was stumbling around, he realized that these may be a good resource in the natural but they were not the right resource provided by God in the present circumstance.

The day would come that David would use armor and weapons such as these, but not this time. David took it off, and as absurd as it may seem, he went out to fight the giant with a slingshot and five stones. This victory would not be won with the expected resources because this was God's fight and David needed to only be influenced by him. We then find that God did provide a sword for David to use to completely destroy the giant with in 1 Samuel 17:50-51.

> 1 Samuel 17:50–51 (NIV84)—So David triumphed over the Philistine with a sling and a stone; without a sword in his hand he struck down the Philistine and killed him. David ran and stood over him. He took hold of the Philistine's sword and drew it from the scabbard. After he killed him, he cut off his head with the sword. When the Philistines saw that their hero was dead, they turned and ran.

At the right time, God gave David a sword—Goliath's. This was the right resource at the right time. This entire story speaks to us about the importance of recognizing the resources available, knowing which ones to use, and when to use them. Just because Saul's armor and weapons were available to David, that did not automatically make them appropriate for the situation he was facing.

God had a different plan and David was wise enough to recognize that. So what did David do? He waited on the Lord. He did what he knew to do—which in this situation mirrored what he had already been accustomed to doing in the field. Stones and slingshots don't normally take down fully armored giants—but God does! Men don't usually kill a lion or bear with their hands—but with God's help David did.

The secret to success is to have the peace in your heart to do it God's way and not your own. For many this can be somewhat confusing. The standard way of thinking is that if I have the resource then I should have the right to use it whenever and however I want. That may be true to some degree, but it is not always expedient. We can get ourselves in a mess when we do the right thing, with the wrong method or with the wrong timing.

Another example of this from the life of David would be the Ziklag fiasco. David was running from Saul and living in the land of the Philistines—the enemy of Israel. David went to battle with them but was turned back because some of the leaders did not trust him. Upon returning to their home base at Ziklag we find in 1 Samuel 30:1-8 that another enemy had plundered the city.

> 1 Samuel 30:1–8 (NIV84)—David and his men reached Ziklag on the third day. Now the Amalekites had raided the Negev and Ziklag. They had attacked Ziklag and burned it, and had taken captive the women and all who were in it, both young and old. They killed none of them, but carried them off as they went on their way. When David and his men came to Ziklag, they found it destroyed by fire and their wives and sons and daughters taken captive. So David and his men wept aloud until they had no strength left to weep. David's two wives had been captured—Ahinoam of Jezreel and Abigail, the widow of Nabal of Carmel. David was greatly distressed because the men were talking of stoning him; each one was bitter in spirit because of his sons and daughters. But David found strength in the Lord his God. 7

> Then David said to Abiathar the priest, the son of Ahimelech, "Bring me the ephod." Abiathar brought it to him, and David inquired of the Lord, "Shall I pursue this raiding party? Will I overtake them?" "Pursue them," he answered. "You will certainly overtake them and succeed in the rescue."

There are two things that stand out to me in this account that are important to this discussion about the Grace Life. First of all, David went back to the Source and took responsibility for his own situational responses. When there was no one left to encourage him, he encouraged himself in the Lord. When all odds were against him, and his own men were talking about stoning him, he picked himself up, dusted himself off, and went to the Source.

This to me is paramount for spiritual victory and success. The fact that he refused to allow the circumstance to discourage him away from God shows his absolute resolve to trust God no matter what. It is at moments such as these, when we don't understand why we are facing the onslaught of defeat that we tend to pull back in doubt. Don't do that! Run to God, not away from him. Go to the Source! Grace is still at work even if your circumstance is rough.

The other thing that stands out to me is that David didn't move until he got the green light from God to do so. Resources surrounded David—men, weapons, anger, adrenalin—but he still asked God if he should pursue the enemy or not. At that, God told him to go after this enemy because he would succeed in the rescue. David and his men pursued and prevailed because they used the right resources at the right time.

Keep in mind that David would not even kill Saul when he had the opportunity to do so—even though Saul was out to kill David. I believe I should say again that just because you have the resource doesn't mean you should take matters into your own hands and use it. God may have something in mind that is all together different than what you are expecting.

I have discovered that there are times when God's perfect will is only revealed through faith and fumes. Don't ever be caught in settling for the convenient "good" when you could have waited for God's best. Faith and fumes doesn't mean you are destitute, it means that you trust God for the full and running over blessing to come from him!

The Grace Life is about divine favor, divine influence, and divine power and not about working under our own thoughts, plans, influence, and strength. When living the Grace Life we learn the great value in fully surrendering to God's purpose and plan. I witnessed the blessing of God through being willing to trust him on faith and fumes. And you will too.

I understand that learning how to follow the leading of the Holy Spirit is somewhat an issue of trail and error, but it is a must. Having the ability to wait when everything in you says, "Jump" is a test of perseverance. But once you learn how to live the Grace Life, you will find peace even when you are running on faith and fumes. *God did that so that I can do this. Then God does that so that I can do more of this.*

Chapter Eleven

FULL AND RUNNING OVER

Having recognized that faith perseveres in times of need and that the Grace Life sustains us through times of faith and fumes, we must now examine the reward of perseverance and faith—abundant blessings! Although there are times when our faith is challenged by needs, God's intent is to pour into our lives his blessings from heaven.

The trip to Bon Weir, Texas was never my favorite idea of a vacation spot. Bon Weir is a very small town just off the bank of the East Texas side of the Sabine River. My uncle and aunt pastored a country Pentecostal church there. In those days there were gardens, pigpens, a lumber mill, deer hunting camps, one little roadside café, and a handful of churches. Although it has been many years since I have visited there, I am pretty sure it has not changed much—if any at all.

Being raised in the big city, this place was like a blast from the past to me. Days in Bon Weir were much slower than those in the Houston area. The nights were darker. It was deep country. For whatever reason, my mom seemed to think that the pastoral parsonage in Bon Weir was a vacation resort. Several times a year we would pile into the car and head over to Bon Weir for our time away from home. This two-hour road trip from Houston seemed like an eternal drive to me as a child.

During at least one of our every year trips to Bon Weir we would experience something different in the form of purple hull peas. Bon Weir wasn't the only place we'd get a sack full of them—the farmer's market downtown Houston had them as well—but Bon Weir was the only place we'd actually sack them ourselves into burlap gunnysacks. I learned a valuable lesson in our pea sacking days. That lesson was simple; "A sack of peas is never full until it is pressed down, shaken together, and running over."

My mom used to say things like, "Get the air out!" because we were buying them by the sack rather than by the pound and she wanted her money's worth. We learned to push, shake, and add peas until the sack was to its "running over" capacity in order to get a lot more peas for the same price as a sack that had not been compressed. It is amazing how much you can add to a sack that you thought was full.

There were times that I thought we were through until momma got a hold of it. Pressed down, shaken together, and running over is an amazing concept. Later I would find that this concept was not new to my mom. It even has a place in scripture in Luke 6:38.

> Luke 6:38 (NIV84)—Give, and it will be given to you. A good measure, pressed down, shaken together and running over, will be poured into your lap. For with the measure you use, it will be measured to you."

In context of this verse, I conclude that the Grace Life is not a life of insufficient blessings. In fact, the Grace Life is a life of blessings that are full and running over. In God we don't receive a blessing that is full of air and empty fluff! God makes sure that when we act according to his favor, influence, and power he returns a blessing to us that is pressed down, shaken together, and running over.

This is why there is no fear in moving into a life that operates in Grace Works. Jesus promised that what we give out of the resources provided to us would be returned—literally poured into our lap—in abundance. Generous giving on our part returns in generous giving on God's part. Looking back to 2 Corinthians 9:10-11 we find this concept clearly.

> 2 Corinthians 9:10–11 (niv84)—Now he who supplies seed to the sower and bread for food will also supply and increase your store of seed and will enlarge the harvest of your righteousness. You will be made rich in every way so that you can be generous on every occasion, and through us your generosity will result in thanksgiving to God.

It is God who supplies the resources to those who sow and then He gives the promise that those who sow reap a reciprocal blessing in their life. God does this in order for us to capture that heart of generosity. It can be no clearer than this: "You will be made rich in every way so that you can be generous on every occasion." The Grace Life is a life of Spirit led generosity. This is the beauty of us allowing grace to direct us in Grace Works activity. We become more like our generous God capturing the very essence of his giving character. It is much easier to walk in Spirit led generosity when you understand the reciprocal blessing of Seed Faith.

Even in times of personal need, we must be sensitive to Spirit led generosity. Several years ago my wife and I were at a minister's conference in Louisiana. This conference was known for taking time during one of the day sessions for the promotion of missionary efforts around the world. To be honest, I didn't go into this service with any thoughts of pitching in because we were in the process of building a gymnasium at our church and finances were very tight. We were even wondering how we were going to pay for things like ball goals, tile, and stainless steel counters and shelves for the new kitchen without going further into debt. Then it happened—Spirit led generosity and the Grace Life.

Sitting in the service I felt impressed to give five thousand dollars to the missions offering. I was hoping that Raylene would argue against this very generous amount considering our situation at home. I turned and asked her if she felt anything and she confirmed the five thousand dollar impression. The funny thing is that she was hoping I felt something much less as well.

With both of us feeling the same thing without communicating it beforehand, she wrote the check. I felt relieved and apprehensive all at the same time. Something in my spirit was leaping in faith while in my flesh I recognized the enormous gift we had just sown.

We had learned to act on Spirit led generosity even though it made no sense in the flesh.

We arrived home on Friday of that week set to reengage with our church building program routine. My mind really wasn't on the missions offering when a gentleman asked for some time with me on Sunday. What happened next was nothing short of amazing. He stepped into my office and said that God had instructed him to give fifty thousand dollars for us to use how we saw fit.

God returned the generous offering ten-fold in less than a week. With that we were able to finish the gym without borrowing another dime! This is the counter balance to faith and fumes—full and running over. Things turned in an instant because while on faith and fumes we were willing to operate under Spirit led generosity. A generous blessing came as a result of generous giving.

A lot of people miss this. Too many times we become stingy with the resources in our lives because we don't understand the power of generosity towards God's Kingdom. I believe that the enemy of the Kingdom propagates this mentality as a means to stop Kingdom Advance. If he can keep the people poor, or if he can stop the resources from passing through them, he can hamper the work of God in the church.

This is evident in so many places. Churches are closing their doors because they can't afford to pay the utility bills and mortgage. Ministry opportunities are being turned down simply because there are not enough finances to do more. This even goes beyond finances.

People can become stingy with their time and talents as well. When people are not willing to give of their time, talent, and treasure, the work ceases to move forward. I need to say clearly that Kingdom Advance requires generosity! The good news is that when we wake up to the Grace Life of generosity we immediately begin to see the reciprocal blessing in our lives.

We were preaching a series of services in Napa, California in the mid-nineties when we watched the fullness of this principle play out in a single mom's life. She told the story that she was struggling to make ends meet during the meetings. She had enough gas and milk to make it a few days and had only five dollars to make it the rest of the week. She knew that she could barely make it stretch until Friday's paycheck, but that was it. An interesting sidebar to this story was that she had been talking to her mom in northern California about the meetings and how God had been speaking into people's lives. At that, her mom refuted this idea by saying that God no longer speaks to people in a personal way.

Sitting in the Sunday service an offering was being taken for us as the visiting minister. Her child reached up and asked what they would be giving in the offering. She tried to ignore this because she knew that there was only a five-dollar bill to last until Friday. How could she tell her child they had nothing to give? Suddenly a divine influence flooded her heart and the impression was clear, *You give me five and I'll give you fifty!*

An internal wrestling match began, as the child also continued to prod by reminding her that the offering plate was getting closer to their row of seats! She felt so compelled by the internal impression that by faith she reached in her purse, handed her last five dollar bill to her child, and watched it go down the row in the offering plate. What you need to know is that whether she knew it or not, she was living in a Grace Life moment. She had the opportunity to follow the favor, influence, and power of God or listen to the voice of fear and doubt. Even though it made no sense in the natural realm, she acted on her faith and surrendered to the plan of God.

Three days later she was rejoicing in the Wednesday night service, telling this story as a testimony of God's reciprocal blessing. On that day, she had received a card from her mom that had been mailed on Monday. Yes, the same mom that just the week before declared God no longer spoke directly to people. In the card she had written, "Don't know why, just because." Along with it was a fifty-dollar check! This young mother's generosity in giving not only opened the door of blessing in her personal financial situation, it also gave God the opportunity to advance Kingdom mentality in her mom.

When the mom heard the story of God saying, "You give me five and I'll give you fifty," she stated emphatically, "Well then, I guess God does still speak to people directly." And he does! This story is another example of God's ten-fold blessing capability. I understand that God is not limited to ten-fold. I have seen full and running over to be less than ten-fold and much higher. Percentage is not what it's about! It's about receiving the right blessing for the right occasion.

Don't be a part of the stingy church! These words may seem harsh yet they need to be addressed. I began full time ministry in 1986. In some regards this was a tumultuous time for those who believe in Seed Faith giving. Multiple scandals had rocked the Pentecostal and Charismatic circles with renowned televangelist making international news with spending extravagance and lifestyle indiscretions. The news hounded the airwaves with the thought that Christian solicitation in the name of the gospel's work was being turned into air-conditioned doghouses (whether true or not), extravagant automobiles, mansions, jet planes, and lifestyles that lacked integrity.

All of this extravagance was being funded by the generous contributions of duped followers. For the record, I have no problem with a minister having nice cars, homes, and even a plane—especially if it is deemed necessary for ministry purpose. The scandals that hit the eighties and even into the nineties spoke more of arrogance, dishonesty, and unscrupulous behavior than they did of ministry importance and personal blessing. Any lifestyle must be matched by a high degree of integrity and character. The lack of integrity and character hinders Kingdom Advance.

I did not have the privilege of being a minister in the pre-scandal years of North American Protestant Christianity. For us, it has been an uphill climb to reestablish faith in the principle of sowing and reaping in the hearts and minds of a lot of people. The financial and character scandals that rocked the church created skepticism that morphed into stinginess. People have found it hard to look past the few—yet notorious—abusers of Seed Faith sowing and reaping to see the vast majority of churches and ministries that don't operate in scandalous fashion. I, along with many pastor friends with high integrity, have had to pastor under the shadow of doubt and skepticism. This shadow has been there even though we have lived far from the scandals being associated with these unscrupulous preachers and ministries.

Human nature reveals that the many are judged by actions of the few in the minds of a lot of people. So we all have to combat the skepticism even though we have never acted without integrity when it comes to finances. I know pastors who won't even take an offering in their services because of this. We all hear about people who tell others that they won't give in the church because they don't want the preacher getting his hands on their money. It is a shame and an attack on Kingdom Advance. It is also contrary to living the Grace Life. The attitude of the Grace Life participant is that if God can get it through me he can get it to me. It then reiterates that concept to declare that when God does get it to me, I will be faithful to get it through me.

I was in conversation with some young adults in our church one time and an interesting comment came up. A young lady made a statement that it would just be awesome if the church had an endowment of money so large that we would never have to receive another offering to pay for the operation of ministry. No sooner than those words came forth, a young man—who just happened to be her husband—said that this was an awful idea. His next words lifted my heart because I knew he understood the Grace Life blessing of full and running over.

He explained to her (in front of us) that if we were to stop giving the people a chance to give to the Kingdom we would be robbing them of their Kingdom blessing. If they never have the opportunity to sow, they will not have the benefit of reaping. This is the beauty of Seed Faith, sowing engages reaping and the reaping is full and running over.

The truth remains that ministries need finances and volunteers to operate. That is the way of the world in which we live. Buildings cost money to build and to operate. It takes finances and people to travel and to put bibles and printed gospel material into the hands of children and adults. The doors of the church cannot open if items such as the utilities, mortgage, and insurance have not been paid. The world operates on a monetary system and there is no way the church can operate around it.

This is why we must have faith in the Seed Faith promise. That is also why we must be individually vested in Kingdom activity. The good news is that God has promised that those who sow towards Kingdom Advance will reap corporate and personal blessings! The corporate blessing is that we get to partake in the activities of the church at large. We are blessed as we see people being ministered to and when we get to enjoy the benefits of corporate activities, ministry, worship, and learning.

It's the individual part that many lose sight of. Catch your focus and see that when you give it is returned back to you. This promise declares that the blessing will be poured into *your* lap, pressed down, shaken together, and running over! There's a "Bon Weir gunnysack overflow" coming your way! His blessings don't come in a "lot of fluff and very little stuff" kind of way. His promise is that the spiritual "sack" containing your blessing has been pressed down and shaken together as to get all of the "air" out.

He then adds the additional blessing of a running over return. In God, you don't just get the sack full; you get what runs over the edge! That is how he turns a five thousand dollar seed into a fifty thousand dollar blessing—full and running over. This is also why we should never be afraid of being generous towards Kingdom activity.

I recognize that I may have said some things in this chapter that could upset somebody, but it needs to be said! I am convinced that there are many people who have been robbed of the full and overflowing blessing because of their lack of faith in sowing and reaping. The modern day church must fight against the spirit of stinginess and follow the leading of God in the Grace Life.

Don't allow the negative voices to convince you that there is no reciprocal blessing in Seed Faith. God has not only promised that your store of seed would be increased, he promised that it would be poured into your lap pressed down, shaken together, and running over.

Have there been times when a ministry or minister has abused and misused the faithful contributions of the people? Absolutely! Have there been churches that got themselves over their heads financially and hounded the people too much for money? Sure there have been! I can understand why certain circumstances have discouraged people from giving. But all of this doesn't disqualify the sound biblical principle that those who give also receive a full and running over blessing!

I said it before and I will say it again, "Don't be a part of the stingy church!" Don't allow the negative voices to steal the joy of giving from you either. Keep in mind that God knows your heart and you will be rewarded for your faithful participation in God's Seed Faith principle. Our reward comes from him! His full and running over blessing is not contingent on who receives the gift and it is certainly not predicated on what they do with it—although I do believe it is important to sow into legitimate ministries who operate with integrity and honesty.

There is something to be said about wise stewardship on our part that seeks to sow into good soil. What I need to clarify is that if the gift is misused for whatever reason, God will deal with them while still giving you the full benefit of faithful service to his Kingdom. Our focus in the Grace Life is on our right actions in cooperating with God's promises and not on the actions of others. When we sow in faith, God knows it and will reward it!

In the end, in order for Kingdom Advance to be realized we need to live lives that are full and running over! Blessed people are the ones who bless the Kingdom of God. The people who have given themselves over to a grace filled generous lifestyle are the same people that propagate the gospel of Jesus Christ. I have heard people say for years that we have been blessed to be a blessing. I believe that more today than I ever have. The grace of God is influencing us to let the blessing flow though us. The church today should be busy building a culture of generosity rather than living in the hole of stinginess.

We should be standing with a generous spirit that is more concerned with what we *get* to give than we are with what we *have* to give. When we understand the full and running over blessing that is coming our way we will no longer begrudge the tithe and offering envelopes and the opportunities to sow. There is no "have to" about it.

There is an overflowing generosity from a full and overflowing blessing. This is where cheerful giving shines as a beacon of light in a dark stingy world. The very essence of the Grace Life is that by God's favor, influence, and power we operate in this world with Grace Works that advance the Kingdom of God. Kingdom Advance should be our motto, focus, and mantra! Kingdom Advance happens in a culture of generosity. I feel like tuning my ears into the voice of the Spirit as he is saying, "You give me five and I'll give you fifty." *God did that so that I can do this. Then God does that so that I can do more of this!*

Chapter Twelve

THE EDGE OF DESPERATION

The Grace Life is fueling us for something big. I mean really big. I am convinced that the mighty work of God is going to explode on the horizon of this generation. Matter of fact, every generation should look for it.

Over the centuries you can see the dramatic impact of grace take shape among the people who were hungry for a divine demonstration. The early church turned their world upside down living in the heart of the Grace Life. The Grace Life was expressed by the Monastic devotees who rose at a time of political and religious corruption to spur the church back towards spiritual disciplines and lifestyle devotion. Martin Luther was saturated by Grace Life when he stood against the legalism and corruption of his day to usher in the awareness of the free righteousness of God that comes without human effort—thus creating the Protestant revolution.

There have been more than one Great Awakenings that brought society to its knees in devotion and repentance to God as the Grace Life exploded among them. The Holy Spirit renewal movements of the Twentieth century brought a new found zeal for the work of the Holy Spirit in the daily life of Christian devotees, inspiring both the Pentecostal and Charismatic awakenings that ushered in a new era for the Grace Life to operate in.

All of these examples and more show that God is highly interested in the hearts of people being stirred for Kingdom Advance through divine favor, influence, and power. It is not enough for us to simply make a confession towards Christ. It is not enough for us to wear the Christian label in word alone. It isn't even enough for us to occupy church pews (or chairs) as a part of our weekly religious devotion.

Although these things are both good and important, they cannot be the total constitution of our Christian experience. Something else needs to happen. Something in our spirit that transforms us into Kingdom Advancers. In all honesty, I have often wondered what that something is. I may not have the total answer even as I write this paragraph, but I do believe I have found an important part of the answer.

In September of 2011, I had the privilege to take another trip to the Philippines with Harvest House International Ministries. I really can't say enough how impacting these trips are on a person's life—especially in the area of stirred passion for the Kingdom of God. It seems that every time I go over there to minister to the beautiful Filipino people they end up ministering to me. The Grace Life Cycle strikes again!

On this particular trip, I could not help but notice how receptive the guests were to the touch of the Holy Spirit at each church and home cell group that we visited. It seemed that at each stop there were people that easily opened up to God's presence and cried out for his touch. This happened even though they had no previous knowledge or religious environment conditioning to do so. We were not telling them to pray this way, we were not coaching them to fully surrender to the moving of the Spirit, and they had never before been a part of something like this demonstrative moving of the Holy Spirit.

Many of these people were from legalistic religious backgrounds that did not encourage personal receptivity to God in this manner. Neither were they accustomed to emotional demonstration during church activity. Yet time and time again, as we would pray for them, they would cry out for God. Many of them were falling to the floor under his power and being baptized with his Spirit instantly.

There seemed to be no walls to break through for divine demonstration among them. There was no need for explanation or coaching. They simply came forward to receive ministry and began to cry out for God's touch and power to come upon them without question. I was so moved by their openness that I inquired to one of the Pastors how could this be. Pastor James is a very special young man of God and I knew he'd have something powerful to say about this phenomenon. What he did say was staggering to me.

"Pastor Rob," he began, "As the Filipino people, we have very little. Our lives are in such a place that we live on the edge of desperation at all times. When these people come forward, they realize that God is really there and that he really hears them. It doesn't take very much to push them over the edge." These words pounded in my heart like a sledgehammer—"We live on the edge of desperation and it doesn't take much to push them over the edge." They echoed through my spirit and ran wild in my mind! I realized instantly that this is the problem for a lot of Christians I know—including myself. We are not desperate enough. Sometimes living in the blessing can knock you off your game.

Having said everything I have about the abundance found in the Grace Life, we must now turn to the balance. The blessings of God can never be allowed to replace the passion for the presence of God in our lives! I made a vow to myself that day that no matter what; I need to live closer to the edge of desperation. Somehow, in the midst of it all, we must become more desperate for him.

This is what the Twentieth century revivalists had. The reformers had it! So did the Monastics and the participants in the Great Awakenings! Taking an honest look at the book of Acts we must declare that this is also what the early church had—they had desperation for God. I believe that desperation is what Paul was alluding to when he instructed Timothy in 2 Timothy 1:6-7

> 2 Timothy 1:6–7 (NIV84)—For this reason I remind you to fan into flame the gift of God, which is in you through the laying on of my hands. For God did not give us a spirit of

timidity, but a spirit of power, of love and of self-discipline.

You may already be aware of the fact that some translations say, "Stir up the gift." Either way, whether stirring or fanning, there is personal action involved with the passion process. In this passage, Paul is clearly telling Timothy not to lose the spiritual passion that had been ignited in his heart at an early age. What we must not overlook is that Paul is placing an emphasis on the fact that the Grace Life comes with an individual responsibility to fan into flame our personal desperation for God.

We need to resolve ourselves to the idea that with divine favor, influence, and power on our side anything is possible. That is, anything is possible if we hunger and thirst for it. The grace of God is influencing us to be desperate for Kingdom Advance. The more we fall under his influence, the more we will desire what he desires and we will love what he loves. This desperate desire is met with an abundant promise in Mathew 5:6.

> Matthew 5:6 (niv84)—Blessed are those who hunger and thirst for righteousness, for they will be filled.

This is exactly what we experienced on that trip to the Philippines. These desperate people became instantly hungry and thirsty for the righteous things of God and they were instantly filled. I think that there are at least two archenemies of spiritual desperation: being too full of everything else and being too self-reliant to express a need for him. I understand that either of these sounds harsh. We may not even mean for either of these to happen. But I have been in ministry long enough to know that these two attitudes create roadblocks for true spiritual desperation.

Dealing with the first, I need to say that I do not believe God has to strip us of everything in order to make us desperate for him. I personally believe that we should be happy and blessed people, and that those blessings should reflect in our lives. God gets absolutely no glory out of his children being down and out. Although we can't compare the blessings in our lives with each other, I do think that whether in America or in a third world country, the blessing of God should reflect in the lives of his children in proportion to the issues and common circumstances of society around them.

With that being said let me point out that if we are so full of everything else, we leave little room for spiritual hunger and thirst. For instance, if our schedule is too full to allow for a time of devotional prayer, then we will not pray. When we do not pray, we forfeit the spiritual benefit that would have come from this time devoted to spiritual communication with God. Many times we simply become so full of everything else that we don't even have room for God. The sad part of that is that we are the ones who lose out in that deal.

Once while preaching in New Brunswick I lived an example of this in the physical world. We were involved in a large conference and had several very busy days of ministry in a row. Between sessions during this conference the host pastor and I took some time to run errands. We then had to get back to his house to settle in for a meal with the ministry team and other conference speakers. This particular pastor's wife was well known for her ability to prepare a wonderful home cooked feast.

As the pastor and I were running errands, she was at the house diligently preparing the meal. It would be a several course meal in which we would eat with real silverware and the finest of bone china. She was pulling no stops on this special occasion. Candles would be lit! Cloth napkins would be placed with crystal glasses filled with southern iced tea arranged in perfect sequence. An exquisite banquet meal awaited us in just two and a half hours.

That is when it happened! The pastor, his son, and I made a decision that would haunt us. It had been several hours since the last time we ate. We had also endured the schedule of morning sessions at the conference and were now running around trying to tie up loose ends for the evening service. As you can probably imagine, we were hungry. Under that condition, we talked ourselves into eating a two-bit greasy hamburger from an international hamburger chain. I'm not talking about a good hamburger. I am talking about the kind of hamburger that is mass-produced and sits for several minutes under a heat lamp.

Do you get the picture yet? Needless to say, the hamburger filled our empty bellies to the point that when we sat for the wonderfully prepared meal, a short two hours later, we were not hungry at all. We settled for the less and had no pleasure in the more! All three of us tried to bluff our way through it, but *she* saw right through our "poker" faces. The fact was that we had no room left to enjoy the banquet because we filled our stomachs with junk food. This reminds me that maybe every now and then we need to de-clutter, or should I say, de-junk. I think that is what Paul meant by "fan into flame the gift."

The Grace Life is a life of spiritual passion. This isn't an issue of things; it is an issue of priority. It's not an issue of having, it is an issue of desiring. God's word is clear that he does not mind us having things. He wants his children to be blessed and for every one of our needs to be met.

What happens in too many lives is that instead of us owning the things, the things own us. Instead of enjoying the benefits of the Kingdom of God we fill our lives with the things of this world. They become the priority instead of God. The opposite of this is that living under God's favor, influence, and power leads us to seek him first as stated in Matthew 6:25-34.

> Matthew 6:25–34 (NIV84)—"Therefore I tell you, do not worry about your life, what you will eat or drink; or about your body, what you will wear. Is not life more important than food, and the body more important than clothes? Look at the birds of the air; they do not sow or reap or store away in barns, and yet your heavenly Father feeds them. Are you not much more valuable than they? Who of you by worrying can add a single hour to his life? "And why do you worry about clothes? See how the lilies of

the field grow. They do not labor or spin. Yet I tell you that not even Solomon in all his splendor was dressed like one of these. If that is how God clothes the grass of the field, which is here today and tomorrow is thrown into the fire, will he not much more clothe you, O you of little faith? So do not worry, saying, 'What shall we eat?' or 'What shall we drink?' or 'What shall we wear?' For the pagans run after all these things, and your heavenly Father knows that you need them. But seek first his kingdom and his righteousness, and all these things will be given to you as well. Therefore do not worry about tomorrow, for tomorrow will worry about itself. Each day has enough trouble of its own.

God knows that we need food, and drink, and clothes. Remember this is just a partial list of felt needs for the purpose of illustration. Nowhere does it say that it is wrong to have these things or even to want them. The point being made is that Kingdom living is seeking God as first priority and understanding that all of these other things will come as well.

When we worry too much about all of the other things we tend to de-prioritize God almost to a place of non-existence. At this, we are no longer living with spiritual desperation. The Grace Life is about fanning into flame our spiritual desperation in order to proclaim, "God did that so that I can do this." The Grace Life is full of divine influence and power that propels us into a life of prioritized focus. We can each make a decision to fan the flame of desperation in our own lives and see our spiritual intensity rise.

The other roadblock to spiritual desperation is a spirit of arrogance that produces a self-reliant attitude. I don't mind admitting that many times this is actually a by-product of bad teaching. When preachers get in the pulpit and demand for people to clean up their act, or place an out of balance emphasis on human effort, it leaves the impression that we have the fortitude to do it on our own. We need to settle the issue once and for all that this is not possible. We need God's help in everything we do. Here is another place to fan the flame.

Spiritual devotions make a huge difference in this arena. The more we humble ourselves in prayer and study God's word, the more we will realize that we need him as an active part of every area of our lives. Self-reliant arrogance is a desperation killer.

Through the years, I have had several people tell me that they will come to church, or live for God, when they get their act together and clean themselves up. I have to stand back and just shake my head at such misled ideology. At no point can we get our act together or clean ourselves up without the mighty work of God in our lives. It's as though we are under the impression that we can actually do this on our own—and we can't. We must be God-reliant and not self-reliant.

I have discovered that if we want to stir spiritual desperation we must do the things that refocus our attention on the things of God. Grace will lead us to this if we will allow ourselves to become sensitive to his leading and prompting. The point here is not to bog us down into some type of legalistic mantra that produces the kind of spirit and attitude that demands desperation or else. The point is to clearly understand that whatever level of desperation we have for the things of the Spirit is up to us.

We must turn every roadblock into a stepping-stone of opportunity by standing firm in God's favor, by following his influence, and by relying on his power. This is the Grace Life in action. It is not my intention to list everything that we could be called to do in the Grace Life but mentioning a few might help you on your journey.

First, we must incorporate into our regular routine the personal practice of devotional and intercessory prayer. Spiritual desperation will never be stirred in a life that is devoid of prayer. I am convinced that the Grace Life produces in us a desire for a prayer life! There is a constant affirmation from God bidding us to join him in spiritual communication. He is calling us to pray. One of the most clear calls from God on the subject of prayer is found in 2 Chronicles 7:14.

> 2 Chronicles 7:14 (NIV84)—if my people, who are called by my name, will humble themselves and pray and seek my face and turn from their wicked ways, then will I hear from heaven and will forgive their sin and will heal their land.

The call is clear that when the people of God make that divine connection in prayer, something powerful happens. This verse alone should be enough to convince us that the grace of God is calling us into a life of prayer.

Relationship requires communication and prayer is the communication conduit between God and his people.

I have stressed many times while teaching on the subject of prayer that relationship without communication is no relationship at all. What would a marriage be like if the couple rarely talked with each other. I would say that it would not be a marriage at all! Matter of fact, I have worked with several couples that had failing marriages and discovered that the main issue that was destroying their relationship was the lack of healthy communication. The only chance of saving the marriage was to help them learn how to communicate better.

I have also seen marriages that seemed to be doomed for failure because of the unfaithfulness of one of the partners come back better than before through open, sincere, and loving communication. If communication is this vital in human relationships we must then admit that our communication with God through prayer is even more vital. Grace is influencing us to pray.

Jesus taught the disciples the importance of prayer on several occasions including the parable of the unjust judge in Luke 18. The gospel writer explains this parable in very clear terms in Luke 18:1.

> Luke 18:1 (NIV84)—Then Jesus told his disciples a parable to show them that they should always pray and not give up.

Notice that the disciples were told to always pray and not give up. When I read that, I immediately see that prayer and not giving up go together like a hand in a glove! If you look at this in the reverse concept you would see that those who are negligent in prayer have the potential to give up. From this we can determine that devotional prayer produces spiritual resolve in the one praying! You've probably heard the old saying, "The family that prays together, stays together." Amend it just a little and you have, "The child of God that prays; stays." Prayer brings strength and resolve.

It is also very easy to see that the law of sowing and reaping applies to prayer just like it applies to other Kingdom actions. When we sow of our time and energy in prayer we reap strength, hope, and spiritual fortitude as well as the answer from heaven. It is clear that the early church understood this concept. I find it interesting that in the Book of Acts history of the church many of the great wonders and miracles happened when they were going to, involved in, or just finishing a time of prayer.

The same is true in the gospels! Here we find that even Jesus had to get away from the crowd and pray. He endured the Garden acceptance of his mission while praying. He prayed on the cross. The importance of prayer is stressed throughout the Old Testament as well. David was a man of prayer. So was Daniel. No lion's den could stop him. The prophets and patriarchs were all people of devotional prayer!

Praying people find it much easier to not give up. Praying people find strength to not quit. It is no wonder Paul stressed this concept in 1 Thessalonians 5:17.

1 Thessalonians 5:17 (NIV84)—pray continually;

This is very simple, yet very profound, advice. In the Grace Life there is a call to prayer that never ceases. Matter of fact, you can literally live in a state of mind that is ever sharp towards prayer. You can pray in an instant because a spirit of prayer resides in you. You may ask, "How can I get a spirit of prayer?" The answer is simple, "Pray often!"

There have been many occasions in my life that I was minding my own business and suddenly felt to pray. Instantly moving into the prayer mode even in restaurants and stores. To me this is what prayer without ceasing is all about. If you have already been in a place of prayer that day, then it is not hard to hear the voice of the Spirit when he says, "Pray now."

That is the Grace Life in action. The Grace Life understanding of prayer is that it is not going through religious motions or some kind of monastic self-discipline. Grace Life prayer is spiritual communication that is divinely influenced and supernaturally charged. That is the call to prayer that I'm talking about. This call to prayer has been witnessed through the years as a place of supernatural impact. If we will listen to the call of the Spirit we will find ourselves being pulled into the realm of the Spirit for divine communication.

I will never forget the time I was called by the Spirit to prayer on a very cold February day in Blacks Harbor, New Brunswick Canada. I was compelled in my spirit to leave the lunch table for a time of intense prayer and found myself caught up in a supernatural moment. I was given a vision where I was standing in the shallow waters of the ocean with a gold coin between my feet.

I wanted to pick this coin up and attempted to do it three times.

As my hand was reaching down a voice boomed, "The treasure is in the deep!" On the third time I stood up and looked towards the open sea. I felt a longing in my spirit to go treasure hunting out in the open water. At that, I came to myself and felt to go to my bible. Opening it, it fell to 1 Corinthians 2:9-10.

> 1 Corinthians 2:9–10 (NIV84)—However, as it is written: "No eye has seen, no ear has heard, no mind has conceived what God has prepared for those who love him"—but God has revealed it to us by his Spirit. The Spirit searches all things, even the deep things of God.

I understood the vision in a flash. The Spirit is calling us to the deep things! Any one of us could be satisfied waking in the realm of a shallow commitment. In the shallows there is less risk and that can be appetizing to the weak at heart. But at the same time there is less opportunity in the shallow waters. God spoke to my heart that day. I could settle for the occasional "coin" that washes up every now and then from the deep treasure, or I could completely sell out and go for the treasure that is in the deep.

It takes commitment and strong desire to go deep sea diving and treasure hunting while to wade along the shore in shallow water doesn't take much effort at all. I made up my mind that day that I was willing to go to the deep. I have since found out that going to the deep means fanning the flame of passion in our heart for the things of God.

The Grace Life is a life of being called to the deep things of God. This takes desperation! This takes a personal willingness and commitment to fan into flame the gift of God that is inside of you! A big part of that is being led into a life of Holy Spirit influenced prayer.

Another way to fan the flame is devotional reading of God's word. We must never forget that in God's word there is life! It is vital to regain the sense of awe and wonder concerning the scriptures. We are blessed to have the written word of God with us. We must also strive to remember, through faith, that picking up the bible is not just reading a book. When we read the word of God with faith, his Spirit begins to illuminate that word with Kingdom awareness and this holy book becomes a source of God's strength, power, and direction. Hebrews 4:12 reveals to us the effect and power of the word.

> Hebrews 4:12 (NIV84)—For the word of God is living and active. Sharper than any double-edged sword, it penetrates even to dividing soul and spirit, joints and marrow; it judges the thoughts and attitudes of the heart.

We have the tremendous opportunity to delve into the word that is living and active. The word of God is not dead literature that is passive in application. It lives, and it works! Even Jesus understood the power found in the word when Satan tempted him in the wilderness. His response to every temptation was, "It is written." What cannot be accomplished on its own can be accomplished through the power of God's word. God has reminded me on many occasions that we need to make sure we have an "It is written" in our vocabulary! What I mean by this is that if we don't have anything else to say we must never forget that speaking the scripture is enough.

It is also true that when we interact with the scripture by faith, the grace of God causes the word of God to come alive in our spirit. As the favor, influence, and power of God show themselves strong in the word, we digest what is written and speak it over our lives. It has been proven many times over that reading, studying, and memorizing the word increases our faith in what God can do. As we read and relive the miracles from the word we realize that miracles are still available today.

We also increase our desire to see his mighty work today as we see the mighty work of the Holy Spirit in the word. If we are going to increase our spiritual desperation, the word of God must live in us. When the word lives in our spirit so does our desire for him. David caught the reality of this in Psalm 119:9-11.

> Psalm 119:9–11 (NIV84)—How can a young man keep his way pure? By living according to your word. I seek you with all my heart; do not let me stray from your commands. I have hidden your word in my heart that I might not sin against you.

David realized that one of the secrets to spiritual success was to place the word of God deeply in his heart, life, and actions. It is clear that a Kingdom lifestyle has the word of God as a part of its devotional inspiration. It is interesting to note how David ties the word in his heart with seeking God with all of the same heart.

The connotation is clear that our hearts engage with the plan, power, and presence of God through the word. Deep inside of us, there needs to be a revival of the word. Take your bible off of the coffee table or nightstand and open its pages! Digest its passages. Commit it to memory. Make the word of God a functioning part of your daily routine.

This reminds me of a conversation I had with a man several years ago. He told me that he had volunteered to clean a church at one point in his Christian journey. While cleaning, he noticed many bibles that had been left on the pews. He said he was so distraught by this that he collected them all and placed them on a table in the foyer with a sign that read, "Please take me home. I'm lonely to be read." This may be extreme, and many of these people may have had other bibles at their house to read, but this is still a good reminder. If we want to stir spiritual desperation, we cannot allow ourselves to neglect God's word. Desperate people hide the word of God in their hearts! This is imperative for Kingdom Advance.

Finally, we must become people of worship. Spiritually desperate people are people of unconditional worship. I believe that God is bringing people to the place of worship where we literally get lost in it. This takes more than a passing glance at the beauty and wonder of God. Desperate people worship with their whole heart.

The Grace Life is a life of joyful adoration and praise given solely to God. It is recognizing the favor, influence, and power of God is our life source! It then becomes easy to worship when we realize that in Him we have everything. I have found it to be true as well that the influence of the Holy Spirit will engage us in a life of worship and praise. In this we find that there is a conscious action that takes place where we become willing participants in praise. Romans 12:1 describes this perfectly.

> Romans 12:1 (NIV84)—Therefore, I urge you, brothers, in view of God's mercy, to offer your bodies as living sacrifices, holy and pleasing to God—this is your spiritual act of worship.

Worship is an act of willing participation as we offer our bodies as living sacrifices to God. A good reminder is that we should never underestimate the power of praise and worship and its impact on our lives. Praise and worship have a way of positioning us into a mindset of God's presence being tangible.

With this in mind, we must never think that praise is only for the good times as a means of thanksgiving for the deliverance or blessings. In the Grace Life we find the strength and fortitude to worship in trying times as well. We must come to the conclusion that praise and worship are influenced by the greatness of God and not by the present position or circumstance. Grace Life people worship regardless of the circumstance and the result is powerful. We are not just worshipping because of what he has done, we are worshipping because of who he is—as revealed in Psalm 100!

> Psalm 100 (NIV84)—A psalm. For giving thanks. Shout for joy to the Lord, all the earth. Worship the Lord with gladness; come before him with joyful songs. Know that the Lord is God. It is he who made us, and we are his; we are his people, the sheep of his pasture. Enter his gates with thanksgiving and his courts with praise; give thanks to him and praise his name. For the Lord is good and his love endures forever; his faithfulness continues through all generations.

As stated before, praising God puts you in the mindset of his presence, which increases the desperation for him. Praise and worship create an "entering into his presence" environment for us to live in. My desire is to get as close to him as I can get—I pray this is your desire too. If we are to increase our desperation we must be people of the presence.

There is a tangible presence of God that must be realized. Some have called this the "manifest" presence and I believe it is important to understand this concept. We understand the omnipresence of God, which simply means he is "everywhere present." God is everywhere, at all times, even if we are unaware of it. It is not as though God shows up in the sense that he has not already been in the room. Some people make this mistake—they think that if they cannot "feel" God then he must not be there.

It is true that works based worship encourages the idea that if we worship enough God will show up but if not, then God will go somewhere else. This idea is ludicrous. I've been involved in church services where the people were told to worship until there was an emotional breaking. They were then told (in essence) that God has now arrived—as though he wasn't there before this demonstrative, emotional breakthrough. I've also heard people say things that insinuated that God's presence lifted off of the people and left because of the lack of performance. This is a ridiculous way to live! God's presence never leaves because he is everywhere present at all times.

What people are confusing is the difference between his omnipresence and his manifest presence. The manifest presence is when he makes himself known in the moment—whether it is a stirring on the inside or even a goose bump on the arm. The manifest presence of God has a way of stirring the emotions, lifting faith, and raising the conscious awareness of the nearness of God in the here and now.

This is what the Filipino people were experiencing when they were proverbially pushed over the edge of desperation. It is a conscious awareness of the reality of God in a tangible form. I have found that all three of these areas—prayer, the word, and worship—are facilitators of getting in a mindset of his manifest presence and create a stirring of the desire for him. When God makes his presence known, our faith is accelerated, and our desire for him pushes past the edge of desperation into a life of Holy Spirit empowerment. *God did that so that I can do this. Then God does that so that I can do more of this!*

THE JOURNEY CONTINUES

As I type, my mind is swirling around the heading typed for this chapter—Conclusion. Conclusion seems like the wrong word when talking about the Grace Life. My mind is not swirling because my labor of love on these pages is drawing to an ending point. Obviously, this particular work must come to an end at some point. It just feels like the word, "Conclusion" doesn't really fit with the idea of the Grace life.

At this, I feel it necessary to subheading this conclusion with the words, "The Journey Continues." The Grace Life will never end for those who have placed their trust and faith in the Lord Jesus Christ. Even in eternity, we will rest in the wonderful favor, influence, and power of Almighty God. What we experience in the Grace Life on this side of eternity is only a small portion of what will be experienced on the other side. Paul described it well in 2 Corinthians 1:21-22.

> 2 Corinthians 1:21–22 (NIV84)—Now it is God who makes both us and you stand firm in Christ. He anointed us, set his seal of ownership on us, and put his Spirit in our hearts as a deposit, guaranteeing what is to come.

What we are experiencing by the work of the Holy Spirit in this life is only a deposit for that which is to come. The Grace Life doesn't end with our life on this earth and that is something to rejoice about. It's pretty cool to think that living the Grace Life is an eternal lifestyle and as a result the benefits of the Grace Life in this physical world are staggering even though they are in a deposit quantity.

Living in the Grace Life increases the level of our Kingdom productivity and really does make us free, fruitful, and forceful participants in Kingdom Advance. To start the process of increasing your participation in the Grace Life you will need to make a commitment to live in such a way as to totally surrender to God's purpose and plan. You also need a willingness to let go of selfish ambition and religious politics. The Grace Life doesn't seek to please people; rather it seeks to please God. The Grace life isn't about rising on the ladder of success in people's eyes and gaining position and recognition.

The Grace Life is about surrendering to God and following his directives in our lives. In the end, only God gets the credit for everything that transpires in and through our lives. God did that! It is only when we humble ourselves to God that we are lifted up by God as Peter states in 1 Peter 5:6.

> 1 Peter 5:6 (NIV84)—Humble yourselves, therefore, under God's mighty hand, that he may lift you up in due time.

The Grace Life declares that God gets the credit when we are lifted up. And lifting up is exactly what will happen to and for you. As I have stated throughout this book, God is interested in your success. He wants you to be productive and to prosper! Happy and blessed for sure! I have come to the conclusion that God gets no glory out of his kids being down and out. The fact is that Kingdom Advance happens with the participation of blessed, happy, and gifted people.

Whatever your gifts may be, God wants to lift you up and give you a place to exercise them for his glory and Kingdom purpose. The multi-faceted act of grace in your life is the fuel behind such lifting. Perhaps the true starting point for many of us is that point of faith that declares, "God wants me to be blessed and happy for Kingdom productivity." I want to declare this emphatically over you. God wants you to live the Grace Life in order for Kingdom Advance to take place all around you. Keep in mind that the final result of the Grace Life working in and through you is Kingdom Advance.

It is here that we discover again that the final result is not final at all. This life never ends! The Grace Life is a continuing journey that passes through this world and into the next. When you live the Grace Life, you are a part of something that transcends time and space with an enormous potential that is out of this world. We are not just meandering through life hoping for an occasional blessing to wash up on the shore. We are people who are filled with the plan, purpose, and provision of God and have become Kingdom Advancers and world changers.

As the journey continues I encourage you to take heart. Know beyond any doubt that God is on your side and that all things are working for your favor according to Romans 8:28.

> Romans 8:28 (NIV84)—And we know that in all things God works for the good of those who love him, who have been called according to his purpose.

When the writer said, "All things" he meant "all things." He didn't say that some things would work for the good or even most things would work for the good, he said all things would! My way of explaining this has been to say that no matter what happens—good, bad, or indifferent—God is working for it to come out in our favor. When living the Grace Life we can't lose! That is a big statement that needs to get in your spirit. You can't lose with God on your side.

You have been called into the Grace Life for Kingdom purpose and the promise to you is that in all things God works for the good. The amazing reality of Kingdom living is that nothing can be against us when God is for us! This is the powerful answer to the rhetorical question asked in Romans 8:31.

> Romans 8:31 (NIV84)—What, then, shall we say in response to this? If God is for us, who can be against us?

Nothing is the answer! I feel compelled to end this volume with some simple advice for activating and keeping active the function of the Grace Life. I have strived through years of preaching and teaching to move away from sermonizing without real life application. I have on many occasions failed in this proposition. It is too easy to tell people what they should do while leaving them perplexed for how to do it. I do not want that to be the story of this book.

If you will give me a few more minutes of your time, I would like to share with you some simple advice on how to keep the Grace Life active on a day-to-day basis. Please understand that I am not attempting to give a lengthy bible study on the subjects forthcoming. We will save that for future volumes and other writers. But I would like to take a moment and give an overview of what activities I have found to be productive in my quest for the Grace Life, knowing that there are other things that can be added as well. You have to start somewhere so here it goes.

The first three were already discussed in the previous chapter and I will give only a reminder here. First, those who truly activate the Grace Life have learned the value of consistent devotional prayer. In simple terms, they have what Christians past have called, "A Prayer Life." I have also discovered that to apply the Grace Life we must learn the value of consistent bible reading and devotional study. We can't accomplish Kingdom work without the Kingdom word implanted in our hearts and minds. Finally, there is the important exercise of devotional worship. Worship creates a Kingdom mindset and a Presence awareness that is necessary for Kingdom Advance through our lives.

Moving beyond these three, another important component of the Grace Life is to have faith-filled fellowship. I can't say enough how important it is to be surrounded with people who are full of faith and have a positive outlook. Whether we like to admit it or not, birds of a feather do flock together! You will ultimately be like the kinds of people you choose to spend time with. I have found it to be true that our choice of companions will impact the effects that the Grace Life has on us.

For example, if grace is influencing you towards faith in a particular circumstance yet you hang out with people of doubt and negative words, the impact of grace's faith will be affected by their negativity. I have had that conversation that stole the thunder of faith in my life. I call them faith thieves—those people who can steal your faith over a cup of coffee or a glass of Dr. Pepper. You know how it goes! You were convinced it would be all right until you went to lunch with that negative voice. Afterwards, you left that table in despair with faith that was in need of repair. Faith-filled fellowship becomes vital in maintaining the Grace Life. Find people who are also living the Grace Life and be a support to each other.

Finally, find a place to plug in and become resourceful in Kingdom activity. I think it goes without saying that I am still an advocate for the local church and its impact on the world. Although the local church has taken a hit of criticism in the last few years, I am convinced that it is still the most viable place for Kingdom resources to be pooled together for Kingdom purpose and advancement.

I encourage you not to listen to the rhetoric that criticizes organized church structures and its attempt to influence you away from meeting regularly as a corporate body to worship and study. Find a church that is filled with like-minded Christians where your gifts can be both utilized and appreciated. Once found, get plugged in. Don't just sit on the sideline seat! Get busy exercising your gifts in the church.

When it comes to finding a church home, some things to look for is to find a church that operates by faith and not by fear, is more interested in people than politics, and one that makes your life better and not worse. One of the most important measuring sticks for a healthy church environment is whether or not the people are empowered for ministry and act as though they are happy to be there.

Another thing to look for is whether it is personality driven with manipulation and legalism or is the focus on Jesus Christ and practical Christian living. You can tell a lot about a church simply by listening to what is being said in and out of the pulpit.

Wherever you choose to assemble for corporate worship, I encourage you to get involved! Don't sit on the sidelines and succumb to consumer mentality! Be a functioning part of the body and exercise your gifts to their fullest potential. The church was never meant to be a one-man show. It is a body made up of many members who are fulfilling their God-given function for corporate life and vitality.

Also be aware of the gifts and callings that are supposed to operate outside of the organized church setting. Kingdom Advance requires us to move beyond the four walls of the church building and into the streets. Plug into a church that encourages its members to be actively involved with ministry to those who are hurting and without Christ in their lives. Your faith and desperation will not grow in a closed minded, stingy church environment that is only concerned with its own needs. There should be a healthy balance between ministry to each other in the church and ministry to those outside of that particular congregation.

The Grace Life is the greatest way to live! It is a life of joy and peace. It is also a life that is free from the bondage of legalism and the fear of manipulation. As you walk in God's grace, you will experience productivity and prosperity like you have never experienced before. Divine favor, divine influence, and divine power are readily available for you, so go for it!

Don't let anything or anyone stop you from experiencing God's best in your life. You and I will live out a testimony that in every situation and under every circumstance God's grace is enough! And to think, we never have to do this thing on our own! *God did that so that I can do this. Then God does that so that I can do more of this!*

ENDNOTES

1   Strong, James. *A Concise Dictionary of the Words in the Greek Testament and The Hebrew Bible.* Bellingham, WA: Logos Bible Software, 2009.

2   Strong, James. *A Concise Dictionary of the Words in the Greek Testament and The Hebrew Bible.* Bellingham, WA: Logos Bible Software, 2009.